SUPPLY AND DEMAND INVESTING

Spotting Imbalances to Find Wall Street's Biggest Winners

A Practitioner's Guide to LSI Charts

Clair Edward Leedom, III

For general information on our products and services, or technical support, please visit www.LSIcharts.com.

To Vali Leedom

And For My Three Girls

Kristina, Emerson & Ellaclair

Acknowledgments

This book would not be possible without the comments, suggestions, proofs, editorial and overall support of so many, not only related to this vast project, but also over many years of working and collaborating with these individuals. I would first like to acknowledge the support of great friends who encouraged and always gave me a shot in the arm to continue onward, including Dale Hendricks, Jon Merriman, James Renner, and Marc Vitolo. The LSI process would literally be a figment of my imagination if not for the programming wizardry of Ken Fayal, who has been with me on this journey for more than twenty years. Sharpening the text of *Supply and Demand Investing* and always available to ping ideas off of was the editorial maven, Michael Burge. I am so appreciative of the many friends who took time to read the manuscript (and, assuredly, the earliest versions were coarse enough to replicate sand paper) and provide thoughtful, insightful, and supremely valued comments and suggestions for this book, especially Alex Woodward, Mike Boroughs, John Park, Frank Fennessey, and Derek Clotfelter. This also includes the unsuspecting guests of my 50th birthday party who were cajoled into departing with the coarsest of early copies to provide feedback. A special thanks to the business newsroom of the venerable *San Diego Union-Tribune*, especially Don Bauder, who gave me two legs to stand on in San Diego, as well as Mike Freeman, Bruce Bigelow, and Brad Fikes. The great team at Van Kasper & Co., particularly Brian Wilhite, Kevin Dede, Adam Dean, Elliot Elbaz, Kevin Director, Alan Auerbach, Jackie Tai, Joaquin Horton, Steve Adams, Billy Brennan, Ken Werner, Denny Anderson, and Mr. Van Kasper. All of the subscribers to *San Diego Stock Report*. My heartfelt thanks to Burton Saft, Christene Renner, Liz Hendricks, David Barnard, George Chamberlin, David Barteld, Mr. Ben Pon, Dick Morrison, Jim Maletis, Dr. Felix Battistella, Rich Hastings, Tim Arthurs, Mike Green and Jim Benham, Dr. Ed Horton, Dr. George Easton, Dr. Esmael Adibi, Frank Mottek, Gar Jackson, Graham MacHutchin, Mike Kehoe, Ralph & Jean Erwin, Rob & Jenna Albert, Lea Clay Park, Jason & Sarah Boyce, Kelly, Mark, and Dick Schwager, Bill Otterson, Levi Hermann, Bonnie Chapman, Buzz Rainer, Ben Doyle, E.E. Reitz, Richard Douglas, Steve Beuerle, Justin Cable, Andrew D'Silva, Ashish Kumar, Michael Mossmer, Jewell and Jade Vitt, Nicolina Pettis, Monte Sahba, Brian Moses, Rowdy Bank, Terry Mims, Tim Cusick, and a host of people I apologize for forgetting. My humble gratitude to Mr. John Bowen. To my father, Captain Clair E. Leedom, Jr., and my sister, Rina Leedom-Graves and the Graves family. Thanks to God for all of the many blessings of family, friends, and the perseverance to complete a truly inspired work.

Contents

Preface

Introduction

Chapter 1

Chapter 2

Chapter 3

Preface

In the 1980s, as a student of the market and novice investor, I would eagerly await the express delivery each night of William O'Neil's Daily Graphs. Daily Graphs was a book of stock charts delivered every night, updating each day's closing price quote. My college budget was never enough to support a full subscription, which was intended for asset managers and serious investors, but every once in a while I would run across a trial subscription rate and sign up for the service.

Combing through the book — which contained hundreds of charts — revealed stocks with share prices that were trending higher (the favorites, of course!), other patterns trending lower, and many stocks that were hard to discern any trend. I had always believed in a special relationship between share price and volume, or number of shares traded, as a means of revealing institutional and the so-called "smart money" movement in stocks. Identifying institutional movement in stocks was important because I believed an investor could capture all of the collective wisdom of their fundamental research and analysis on a particular stock. I told myself that if the institutions were buying the stock it would have to be manifested through an increase in volume. I would look specifically for charts with a recent jump in share price and volume, thinking institutional investors were buying these stocks that were ready to break out to higher prices. However, with the share price pattern displayed at the upper part of the chart and volume represented as a bar graph at the bottom of the chart, it was always difficult for me to "see" how volume may, or may not, play a role in price movement. Arming myself with a ruler, I would try to align price changes with the volume on the bar graph at the bottom of the chart, to verify that the two coincided. Did a jump in share price coincide with a similar rise in the day's number of shares traded of the stock? Thus, my excitement for the evening was set with the thought that I would discover the next major winner by locating those charts that showed a big rise in price and volume.

Alas, things never quite go as planned. Not that the theory of a price-volume combination was flawed; it was that there were so many candidates to choose from that I could never seem to pick the right one. When I did finally pick a stock that appeared to have all of the right characteristics, it always turned out to be the wrong one while I watched other stocks soar. Why did one stock surge to new highs while another one that looked virtually the same on the chart peak right after I bought it? Was my stock in the wrong industry group, contain inferior financials, or face some unforeseen competition compared to the others? Or was it something more nebulous to me, such as a lesser rival buying the stock as opposed to a Fidelity or T. Rowe Price? And, more depressingly I thought, wasn't I really just following the herd anyway, because so many other investors were looking at these same stock charts? I could find no answers to reverse my futility. However, out of these ruins began the odyssey that eventually led to the creation of the process that is the subject of this book.

While I was learning the hard lessons of the market during this experience, there was one aspect that fascinated me about those price and volume charts that I pored over each night. As I slid my trusty ruler across the volume bar at the bottom of the chart, I would wonder if there was some sort of break point for trading volume that made a particular price movement more relevant that day than on other days. In other words, exactly how much volume was enough volume? Was it simply that the higher the volume bar the better the stock would perform? Should I then only buy those stocks with the tallest bars? Or was it possible, conversely, to have too much volume, where there was just too much interest in the stock? In other words, was the cat already out of the bag by the time I "discovered" this trend? These perplexing questions had to have an answer, and I believed that by solving them I might actually end up buying the right stock for a change.

My fascination with volume was centered on a very simple premise that anything carrying a floating price has to be derived through the market driven dynamic of supply and demand. Should it be any different for a stock as compared to say, oranges sold at the corner market? The stock market should actually be the best measure of supply and demand, considering that all of the buyers and sellers had only one central marketplace in which to trade, versus a commodity like oranges, which were available in every corner market and subject to so many regional variables. Therefore, taking Disney as an example, if it had a different price close each day, it must obviously be set by the forces of supply and demand. And at each new day of trade the sellers (suppliers) would lock horns with the buyers (demanders) in a battle that determined whether the stock finished higher or lower. Though this basic observation would not sound any alarm bells in the annals of discovery, it created a new mindset for me to consider volume. And based on my meager trading results to date, it was actually a breakthrough.

By taking my thought one step further I deduced that a typical day's change in price for Disney, for example — up $2.00 on 10 million shares traded — could be considered the resulting statistical "supply and demand outcome" for the day. In other words, the forces of offsetting supply and demand generated 10 million shares of volume and, as a result, produced a $2.00 net gain in the stock. Based on this fact, I could then consider the day's change in share price and volume to be related, meaning they were a function of each other. In retrospect, maybe I never needed to line up my ruler against the volume bar in the first place, as those singular volume bars were irrelevant if not considered in the context of change over time and as a function of associated share price movement. This led me to consider what a stock chart would look like if the volume bar was replaced by a collective representation of changes in price and volume over time, or a "supply and demand summation" line, alongside each day's closing price. Wouldn't this type of chart provide a far more useful view to spot how institutional and smart money activity influenced price movement, as opposed to a one-dimensional volume bar? With my own alarm bell ringing, the line representing "supply and demand," or Leedom Strength Indicator (LSI), was eventually born and is revealed today in this book and through LSIcharts.com. Over the pages that follow I look forward to bringing the LSI chart process and associated patterns to life for investors as the key to finding the next major winners in the stock market.

As a postscript to readers, LSI from its inception was meant to indicate the underlying "strength" of the stock through supply and demand. After using this abbreviation for more than 20 years I found it was nearly impossible to refer to it by any other name and something that might sound more modern or relevant for this book. In the end, I knew if I made a change I would only end up repeating "LSI" after saying it for so many years, rendering any new, possibly more relevant acronym moot. Thus, LSI it is and remains and the mysteries behind this analysis are revealed over the chapters that follow.

Introduction

Objectivity is a most cherished virtue of investors. The most successful investors in history were, whether even they knew it or not, also some of the most objective when considering the wide range of investment opportunities available. Too many influences tend to chip away at our objectivity when it comes to investing, marginalizing our independence and driving us toward the dreaded herd. These influences unintentionally impair our judgment and lead us down a precarious investment path. The primary difference between the Warren Buffets of the world and the majority of investors is the ability to remain objective.

But how do we, as investors, effectively retain our objectivity and avoid herd mentality? How do we channel our emotions, dispositions, and analyses to approach each investment dispassionately and escape costly biases? Perhaps, by revisiting our analogy of oranges at the corner market from the Preface, we can draw a familiar distinction. How is it we can objectively avoid paying top dollar for a bag of oranges only to turn around and emotionally pay top dollar for a hot stock? Consumers often complain bitterly when confronted with higher prices for items like produce, to the point of leaving them on the shelf or choosing an alternative rather than paying a higher price. This is a rational, objective mindset we have acquired over many years of buying everyday items such as oranges at the market. While we understand the impact on orange prices from short crops as a result of frost, or large bumper crops, we intuitively sense when prices are too high or, conversely, so low we feel like squeezing our own orange juice. Our objectivity when it comes to everyday items is pretty close to absolute. Yet, this same objectivity doesn't seem to apply when it comes to stocks. In fact, the prevailing mentality typically is that the higher a share price goes, the more a stock becomes coveted by investors. In a strange twist of logic, investors tend to think the price of a surging stock can continue upward forever. It's hard to feel that way about a bag of oranges! In similar fashion, the more a stock goes down, the more we seem to be relieved at having avoided it, often without regard to a potentially attractive valuation. Of course, oranges and stocks are two entirely different considerations, but our inability to remain objective with stocks is based, in large part, on the influence of emotions. If we could consider stocks under the same mindset of supply and demand that influences the price of oranges, we might just feel differently about paying top dollar …

Investing emotions are not something that we need to fix, but merely channel. I was always amused by those who said investors need to confront emotions by "thinking differently" or "outside the box" when it comes to the stock market. Just how does one think differently? Can we actually reroute the circuitry in our brains to produce different outcomes? And exactly what is this box that we supposedly need to escape from? Maybe if someone just yelled, "Stop doing what you are doing!" we could understand much more clearly what they meant. As a social species, we are destined to the same recurring outcomes our brain circuitry is designed to provide us. It should be of little wonder then that there is a herd mentality when it comes to investing and that we all tend to make similar mistakes. Improving our investing by trying to change our brain function is an effort in futility. And that is not to say our circuitry is errant; it has gotten us this far, hasn't it? But if we could become more objective about our investing and apply the same mindset we use when purchasing a bag of oranges, it could change our outcomes without the need for new wiring. I recall a friend who had lost on so many stock trades that he deduced he should actually buy whenever he felt the urge to sell. A good theory maybe, but it didn't sound like a confident way to get through life. However, if he could adjust his inputs to channel the emotional aspects of his thinking and reasoning, maybe he could make better decisions.

And emotions are not the only hazard confronting our objectivity; a good many predispositions weigh on us, as well. Unlike emotions that we tend to "kick ourselves" over, we actually embrace our predispositions. Our library of collective investing factoids acquired over the years, such as "never invest in stocks tied to commodity prices," or "avoid money losing biotechnology stocks," empower us to feel that our experience will contribute to improved outcomes. While there are clear benefits to market experience, predispositions can also prevent us from taking advantage of important opportunities. During the 2008 housing crisis, how many times were investors told to avoid Home Depot stock because the consumer was overextended, underwater, and essentially incapacitated from a purchasing perspective? Though these facts were relevant at the time, we also knew problems facing the consumer wouldn't last forever. How could we turn this predisposition switch off at just the right moment to objectively consider Home Depot stock? *Supply and Demand Investing* introduces the concept of LSI to counter our emotions and predispositions, and consider investments from a purely objective supply and demand perspective. Instead of focusing on the growing despair of the consumer inculcated into our heads by every major publication and media source, we could ask ourselves why institutional investors were starting to take positions again in Home Depot shares.

Another key aspect of investing that tends to limit objectivity is our analysis. While this may seem like a contradictory statement — after all, investing the time to get to know a company is an inherently important task — our analysis, generally speaking, is often tied more subjectively than objectively to historical facts. I would certainly never disagree with an investor who selects companies based on such metrics as leading market share position, competitive advantages, and strong growth in revenue, earnings, and free cash flow. But I would disagree that these facts alone imply that a stock should trade higher. Another investor could equally argue that this information is already quantified and reflected in the current price of the stock. Having spent many years as an analyst for a sell-side investment firm, I understood the power of forward analysis in researching stocks. I wrote research and formally covered ten companies, living and breathing those ten companies daily, for several years, to the point where I felt as if I could anticipate what management was going to do next. As we all know, it is not what a company actually reports during its earnings release, but what is said about the future. It was my job to understand what the future held. An investor who studies numbers without an eye toward the future is like a pilot focused on air speed without regard to the mountain ahead. Of course, there are the "deep dive" investors, like a Jim Chanos, who can glean nuggets out of financial statements to unmask the Enrons and Worldcoms of years past and find the Apples and Googles of the years to come. But the majority of investors may lack the time or experience to conduct this type of rigorous analysis, especially when trying to cull selections from a large number of stocks. How, then, can we focus our analysis to become more effective in identifying the right companies?

Every day in the market, behind the hundreds of millions of shares traded on Wall Street, brokerage and investment banking firms are interacting with mutual and institutionally managed funds to disseminate research and generate trading opportunities. This interaction is largely responsible for the day's up and down price blips in stocks. Unfortunately for investors, there is no drop down menu on *Yahoo Finance* that allows us to find out the reason behind the daily blip in share price, although we would all surely love to know. As an analyst, it was my responsibility to talk to company management, vendors, suppliers, and even other investors to continually gather information and stay current on my coverage list of companies. For Callaway Golf, a company I covered as an analyst, I would spend a good deal of my time calling retailers across the nation to find out how a new driver, such as the Hawk Eye, was selling. For a healthcare informatics company like Cerner, an analyst team might interview hospital IT managers, speak to physicians, and attend various vendor conferences to find out how a new medical enterprise solution was performing. A fortunate analyst might learn that a major hospital group was replacing an existing enterprise system in favor of adopting a Cerner solution. This nugget of actionable information would then be directed to the firm's clients who owned Cerner. This is the real story behind many of the price blips in stocks each day on Wall Street. Analysts gather important pieces of information, write a report, and disseminate the information to clients of the firm who are fund managers in charge of billions of dollars for investors. This collective information, gathered by the thousands of analysts across the nation covering individual stocks or sectors at both the brokerages as well as in-house at mutual funds, is responsible for generating the lion's share of the day's up and down price changes in stocks.

Not to imply that following analyst reports is the best way to gain an edge in the market. What should be evident, however, is the power of forward analysis as the primary mechanism that leads fund managers to bid stocks higher in anticipation of future results. If our prototypically ideal stock — which features leading market share, competitive advantages, strong growth in revenue, earnings, and free cash flow — shows evidence that this trend is likely to accelerate, then I would agree the stock is probably undervalued and should trade higher. Is there a way we can acquire this institutional insight without quitting our day job and performing all of this forward analysis ourselves?

Many investors track the holdings of mutual funds to find out what they are buying and selling in an attempt to gain these insights on particular stocks. Institutional investors and mutual funds must report their stock holdings each quarter to the Securities and Exchange Commission through 13-F filings. While this is a great source of information for those trying to find out what stocks their favorite fund manager has purchased, the problem is that these funds do not have to report their holdings until 45 days after the close of each quarter. By the time we know Fidelity or Janus has taken a position in Netflix, for example, it is possible they could have completely sold out of the stock (which we wouldn't know for a further 45 days). And then just how valuable is it to know that it was Fidelity buying over another large firm when they own thousands of stocks? Do they really love Netflix, or are they merely buying it to add exposure to a certain sector? It is hard to tell. On the trading desk of the firm I worked for it was a closely guarded secret when a fund manager was taking a position in a covered stock, not even the analyst was privileged to know (although we always suspected!). *Barron's* Roundtable provides a great annual discussion of the favorite stocks of prominent investment managers and advisors, though I can assure you these are stocks that they had already bought, not ones they were in the process of buying. Knowing who is buying a particular stock is nice information to have, but its relevance is debatable considering the time lag involved. Instead of knowing *who* is buying, it is far more important to know *when* institutions are buying to gain our insight.

While we certainly know that institutional investors are not right all of the time, their importance is derived from the substantial buying and selling power they possess. According to the subject of this book, institutional investors collectively have the power to create imbalances in the supply and demand equilibrium of a stock that can influence its future share price. Just like the impact of a short crop on the supply of oranges that push prices higher, the buying power of institutional investors can similarly affect the existing supply of a stock and impact its share price. Are more funds buying than selling to create a demand imbalance, or are they locked in an indecisive tug-of-war? The share price of a stock may reflect the outcome of this activity, but the juicy statistics that can influence future share prices are buried within the changes of price and volume. *Supply and Demand Investing* guides investors on how to "see" these institutional forces at work, in a pure supply and demand scenario, before their influence on share price has been realized.

One of the most popular methods used by investors to gain insight into the buying and selling trends of institutional investors to predict future share prices is stock charting. Also known as technical investing, stock charts have long dominated the investment landscape, and their influence upon investing is without question. They are easy to access, easy to read and, in the end, have become a rather simple means for investors to "conduct analysis" on a stock. Stock charts have, in many ways, become the tool of choice in an attempt to capture the meticulous research and analysis taking place in the market that underpins share prices. I have heard many times that stock charts represent the collective wisdom of investor sentiment, as all of the news and information available is reflected in each day's closing price. Hundreds of books have been written on the subject, with varying opinions on how to buy and sell stocks, as well as the specific trend lines to identify. And it is virtually impossible to avoid looking at stock charts as they are found everywhere, from *Yahoo Finance* to *Google Finance*, to a host of professional websites such as Stockcharts.com. Just like a sports fan constantly checking the scoreboard during a basketball game, the ultimate scoreboard for investors is a company's share price. It is the final arbiter of pleasure and pain in the stock market.

However, if it is true that all of the news and information is reflected in each day's closing share price, how can stock charts be effective as a predictive tool? The closing price of the previous day, month, or year should be no more a predictor of the next day's closing price than any other price. In addition, if so many investors are using stock charts to make investment decisions, how does one analyze a chart better, or more profitably, than the next investor? Aren't we all looking at the exact same thing? I remember a colleague who specialized in stock charting confiding to me during a particularly rough stretch in the market, "Stock charts work really well … until they don't." What he was saying, of course, was that as long as the trend held, everything was just fine.

LSI challenges the pervasive notion of stock charting as a predictive tool for investing. The future share price of a stock is simply not possible to deduce from the historical price trend without an understanding of the forces that collectively influence it. LSI "unlocks" these collective forces to reveal imbalances upon supply and demand created by institutional investors. Investors can now analyze institutional trends directly alongside changes in share price, in contrast to the one dimensional view provided by a stock chart. An interesting comment on stock charting came from a fund manager that I used to call on as an analyst. He once boasted to me that he didn't follow stock charts, "he made them," meaning that the buying power of his firm alone could change the course of a stock, so why would he ever look at a chart? At the time, I smiled at his boast thinking, "Give me a break …" but I never forgot it due to the audacity of such a statement. Today, while the high frequency and algorithmic traders might take exception to the claim, his comment is actually quite true when placed into the aggregate of funds buying or selling a particular stock. It serves as a rather colorful reminder of the capacity of institutional investors to create imbalances that influence share prices.

In the end, nothing imperils the objectivity of investors and drives the phenomenon of herd mentality in investing more than following the price of a stock on a chart. By using stock charts, an investor's eye is ultimately trained to find "the great looking chart" and thus, avoid "the terrible looking chart." It is not hard to deduce that the great looking chart is likely to be a stock that has gone up a lot, and the terrible chart is a stock that has probably dropped quite significantly. Which formations would you believe stock chartists are likely to consistently buy? Certainly not those among the terrible looking charts … just think what their investor friends might say! Recalling our discussion of emotions and brain circuitry, it is simply our human nature to buy those stocks where all of the action appears to be positive and avoid what inherently appears to be heading toward zero. It is the reason stocks can rise to extreme valuations and fall to such extreme depths. Add to that the splendor and excitement of a great looking stock chart and it becomes an epic battle to fight the mentality of the herd urging us to pay top dollar. That is not to say great companies do not continue to be great investments and shouldn't be bought at ever higher prices. Just look at the stock of Church & Dwight. The key, however, is holding onto our objectivity when our eye is trained to focus on those stocks that keep rising.

Under LSI analysis, the definition of a great looking chart and terrible chart becomes far different. *Supply and Demand Investing* outlines an entirely new way of looking at stocks, effectively bringing to light the volume and related price changes that are obscured in stock charts. What if a stock that is hitting new highs on a price chart is also developing a contrary supply imbalance? Would we still rush out to buy this stock? Chances are we would perform far greater due diligence on the company to investigate this negative fly in the ointment. LSI indentifies these particular patterns as negative divergences where a rising share price clashes with a supply imbalance to flash a danger signal. If we can't change our brain circuitry concerning the "great looking stock," maybe through LSI we can now at least "think differently" about our potential investment. After all, who wouldn't find value in knowing the collective institutional investor sentiment of a particular stock before rushing out to buy it?

Supply and Demand Investing educates investors on the LSI process through each of the book's three chapters. Imagine the value of being able to look at the unique supply and demand characteristics of your own stocks to identify existing imbalances? Chapter 1 covers the key LSI chart patterns to guide readers on how to identify the presence of supply and demand imbalances. Investors can learn how to identify favorable investing environments for their own stocks through demand imbalances, as well as spotting unfavorable environments that are under the influence of a supply imbalance. Individual LSI charts are available to investors separately from this book at LSIcharts.com. Chapter 2 outlines specific patterns and provides analysis to identify buying opportunities in stocks using LSI charts. From power patterns to more conservative formations such as Bowls, investors can use LSI charts to determine patterns that indicate the beginning stages of future share price gains. Finally, how do we put LSI charts to work in our own investing?

In Chapter 3, investors can explore various trading and investing strategies using LSI, and learn how to build portfolios by selecting stocks with specific imbalance patterns. Chapter 3 concludes with three unique case studies of portfolio managers that have successfully implemented LSI charts into their own professional investment strategies.

By focusing on imbalances of supply and demand it is possible to channel our emotions, predispositions, and analysis to become far more objective in deciding which stocks to buy and sell. LSI provides this capability and, in the chapters that follow, guides investors on not only how to gauge institutional activity in stocks, but how to use this information to make investment decisions. We'll reveal in the chapters ahead that when institutional investors are moving in unison to buy a stock, their collective influence on share prices can be explosive.

Let's get started!

Chapter 1

An Introduction to LSI

The forces of supply and demand touch all aspects of our society, from the price of a jet airplane to the price of a paperclip. And whether you are buying gasoline at the local service station or selling items on eBay, you will be subject to the influences of supply and demand. Higher gas prices typically occur during the summer driving season when interstate highways are filled with vacationers. Or when trying to sell a collectable we often hear the refrain: "Those are not very popular right now …" We can thank Adam Smith and a host of other economists for this.

For investors, however, the laws of supply and demand can be much harder to quantify. Of course we can see stock prices go up and down in the market, but the forces driving these moves are often obscure. Add to that the more recent phenomena of high frequency trading, dark pools, and algorithmic trading — all occurring with light speed efficiency — and it becomes harder still to associate the actions of buyers and sellers. But even with these influences there is the fundamental market dynamic of a buyer meeting a seller to establish a price. There is still Fund A seeking to buy stock XYZ, and Fund B seeking to sell stock XYZ, with traders at investment houses in the middle working the phones to negotiate prices. These forces influence share prices in a market environment according to the laws of supply and demand. But is it possible to actually see these forces at work?

The Leedom Strength Indicator, or LSI, provides just such a tool for investors to see the influences of supply and demand upon stocks. LSI works by revealing the secretive and hidden influences on supply and demand created by institutional investors. Here's a simple supply and demand example to understand how LSI works. A small investor buying 100 shares of IBM at a specific price can create demand, but with an average daily trading volume of six million shares, those 100 shares are easily supplied and the trade will have no influence on IBM's share price. But what if a buyer demands two million shares — the equivalent of 33 percent of the day's average trading volume? On a normal day the six million shares traded are split roughly equally between buyers and sellers at three million shares. An additional two million shares would mean roughly five million shares of demand from buyers against three million shares supplied by sellers. Assuming no unusual market conditions or news from the company, IBM shares will likely move higher to meet this excess demand. More shares need to be supplied to complete the trade, with higher prices serving as the motivation for sellers. In this simplistic example, the forces of supply and demand would dictate a higher price for IBM that day.

Taking this example one step further, let's imagine that an external event, such as an increase in global growth expectations, leads several institutional investment managers to decide they want to own IBM to take advantage of this anticipated growth. These managers each demand two million shares of IBM to add to their portfolios, resulting in higher than average trading in IBM with a bias to the demand side. However, all of these new buyers would need to pay significantly higher prices upfront to purchase IBM shares, as an average three million shares per day in supply volume would be unable to satisfy this new demand. The alternative for these new investors would be to stretch their purchases over a period of time in an attempt to take advantage of periodic price declines. This new demand stretched over time would create a sustained period of buying, or demand in the stock. In this simple example, IBM shares would trade higher every time the volume is above the average six million shares due to an excess of buyer demand against a consistent supply of three million shares per day. Thus, we see an uptick in volume resulting in a positive change in share price. For the price to fall against a consistent supply we would need to see fewer than the three million shares of demand for the day, as the new buyers "take a break." Therefore, we would see up days in IBM shares on higher than the average volume of six million shares, and down days in the stock on lower than average volume.

Of course the stock market is much more complex than our simplistic supply and demand example of IBM. There are thousands of buyers and sellers each day in widely held stocks and it is rare to be able to attribute price gains to just one or two buyers. Regardless, the overall laws of supply and demand support this view, as a survey of price and volume data over time shows that stock prices trend consistently higher on the majority of days when trading volume is above average. LSI provides investors with the ability to gauge this activity to identify favorable buying and selling environments in stocks.

Revealing Institutional Trends: Imbalances of Supply and Demand

LSI is an investment process originally developed in 1992 that is used to find stocks poised for significant price movement based on imbalances of supply and demand. These imbalances are produced mainly by institutional investor buying and selling patterns. The power of the LSI process is its ability to interpret volume and share price changes and correlate them as a function of supply and demand. Investors use LSI chart patterns to find stocks with imbalances that correspond to major share price movement.

How does LSI identify these imbalance situations? Imbalances are created by a recurring pattern of upticks in volume that result in share price change. These individual upticks are called "**pulses**," and they are caused predominantly by institutional investor buying and selling. Institutional investors moving into or out of stocks produce volume and share price changes that fall well outside the normal averages as calculated over time. For example, if the average trading volume of a stock is 500,000 shares per day, a two million share day would be more meaningful, particularly if it resulted in a significant change in price. From a supply and demand perspective this buyer, or "demander," would influence the share price if they were to buy a larger number of shares than the average supply of stock typically offered in the market (as described in our earlier example of IBM). Major volume and price changes alter the supply and demand equilibrium, creating imbalances that vary in intensity over time. However, to the normal investor these imbalances are not readily evident, and LSI brings them to light through specific patterns on the LSI chart. These patterns are formed by "**spikes**," or vertical upward or downward jumps on the chart, indicating an imbalance. By uncovering imbalances through spike patterns, investors can now truly harness the power of supply and demand.

LSI Basics
What You Need to Know to Get Started

The LSI Algorithm

At the heart of the LSI process is the LSI algorithm that processes pulses, volume and share price changes in individual stocks, and interprets them into readable chart patterns. As we have discussed, these volume and share price changes identify the presence of supply and demand imbalances that are the key to identifying institutional activity. Patterns appear along the LSI line as generated by the algorithm, which is a summation of the supply and demand trend. The LSI line is visible in one-year (daily) or five-year (weekly) views alongside the underlying share price of a stock on an LSI chart.

    The LSI algorithm works by formulating a unique multiplier based on pulses for each stock on a daily or weekly basis. The multiplier is determined by the deviation of volume change, as well as the share price change, from trailing averages — the duration of trailing averages is also determined by the algorithm — to reveal imbalances. The higher the deviation from averages, the larger the value of the multiplier that is formulated by the algorithm. Although there are significant complexities involved in identifying and analyzing individual pulses that make up the proprietary LSI algorithm, a simple way of understanding how the algorithm generates spikes is from the following illustration. Suppose the volume of a stock on a particular day is four times its trailing average. This would lead the algorithm to produce a daily volume multiplier of 4.0. If the associated daily share price change is $2.00, a spike of magnitude $8.00 would appear on the LSI line. The math is simply: 4.0 (volume multiplier), multiplied by $2.00 (share price change), to equal $8.00. (Note, the multiplier of share price change is based on volatility and the deviation of historical average price changes, but for simplicity we are using the actual daily price change of the stock in this example.) On a daily LSI chart, a spike of $8.00 would appear on the LSI line in relation to the $2.00 rise in the closing share price. On the LSI line, higher than average volume and price change would produce a spike, whereas average or lower than average volume would result in flattish line behavior. Spike magnitudes can therefore vary based on multiplier values, but when viewed over time they provide powerful patterns that reveal the size of an imbalance (See Table 1).

Table 1	LSI Algorithm Spike Magnitudes			
Spike Magnitude	LSI Multiplier	Price Change	The Result of ...	Spike Type
$0	0	$2	Volume within averages	None
$8	4.0	$2	Volume 4 times trailing averages	Primary
$20	10.0	$2	Volume 10 times trailing averages	Major

Imbalances of supply and demand that develop over a period of time result in multiple spikes on the LSI line that resemble steps (See Figure A). These spikes form patterns on the LSI line that will be illustrated later in this chapter. Periods of imbalance are usually driven by active institutional investor buying or selling trends, with larger imbalances tending to have a greater future impact on share price. Some of the most dramatic spike patterns on an LSI line are associated with stocks that are undergoing a material change in their institutional ownership base. Imbalances that develop in stocks that are not widely owned by institutions can produce vivid and sometimes explosive spike patterns, called **"Ladders"** and **"Waves,"** which we'll discuss later in this chapter.

Figure A. Spikes on the LSI Line forming Classic Stair-Step spike patterns

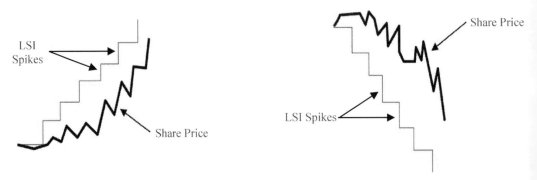

Stocks of large companies, such as those of the Dow Jones Industrials or S&P 500 indexes, tend to have significant pre-existing institutional ownership, resulting in a rarity of major long-term supply and demand imbalances in these stocks. This large percentage of institutional ownership corresponds to far more subtle movement of the LSI line. As we describe in the chapters that follow, large stocks with a high percentage of existing institutional ownership are best viewed using daily LSI charts to identify imbalances, as opposed to the longer-term oriented weekly charts recommended for the majority of other stocks. Daily LSI charts have a greater sensitivity to imbalance trends than weekly charts due to their short-term view, allowing investors to pick out these more subtle trends. It is noteworthy that in certain infrequent circumstances, price changes occur on such low volume compared with the average that the LSI line can actually move in an opposite direction to the underlying price change. These price changes reflect the lack of any substantive supply and demand imbalance and are associated most commonly with low price/low volume stocks.

As institutional investors interact uniquely in all stocks, the LSI line is equally unique and serves as a kind of fingerprint of each company's respective supply and demand characteristics. And similar to the analysis of fingerprints, specific identifiers or patterns that are common to all LSI lines offer the opportunity for investment analysis. For example, an LSI line that is relatively flat over a period of time indicates an overall equilibrium of buyers and sellers in the stock. However, LSI lines that show significant vertical spike patterns indicate the presence of major supply and demand imbalances. For this reason, the LSI line can be thought of as a "supply and demand summation" of the underlying stock. When imbalances build to form specific LSI patterns, investors can take advantage of these patterns to make buy and sell decisions.

LSI Spike Formations

The underlying strength of a supply or demand imbalance in a stock is revealed by the magnitude, or length, of spikes on an LSI line. Spike magnitude is determined by the LSI algorithm based on multiplier values. These spikes, in order of increasing magnitude, are referred to as micro, minor, primary, major, and rare spear spikes as outlined in Table 2. Spikes occurring in formations of two or more create actionable LSI patterns closely watched by investors to reveal buy and sell signals. These patterns are illustrated through a multitude of examples later in this chapter.

The following LSI chart illustration of Apple (Chart A) provides our first look at these spikes as they occur along the LSI line as well as the relevant features of an LSI chart. Over the course of this book we will describe and categorize key patterns of these spikes that readers will become increasingly proficient in identifying through the subsequent chart examples.

Table 2	LSI Spike Formations	
Spike Name	**Description**	**Frequency**
Micro	Very small magnitude, 10% or less of primary spike magnitude	Common
Minor	Small magnitude, 50% or less of primary spike magnitude	Common
Primary (Common)	Spike magnitude ranging from 1-2x the share price of the stock	Common
Major	Large magnitude, 150-200% of primary spike magnitude	Infrequent
Spear	Exceptionally large magnitude spike causing a chart distortion	Rare

LSI Chart First Look: Apple

Investors use LSI charts to make investment decisions based on institutionally driven imbalances of supply and demand. LSI charts depict both the share price and LSI line of the underlying stock over one-year (daily) or five-year (weekly) time frames. Investors scan these charts looking for known spike patterns that indicate the presence of imbalances. These patterns along with variations of spike magnitude are essential to understanding the strength of an imbalance to gauge the aggressiveness of institutional buying or selling. According to LSI rules outlined in Table 3, spike patterns can indicate whether a stock is an immediate investment opportunity or candidate for future action.

Before we begin learning the specifics of what an investor looks for on an LSI chart, there are basic aspects of the chart that require understanding. Chart A depicts a highly

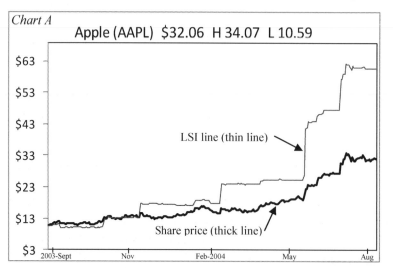

positive one-year daily LSI chart of Apple, indicating a major demand imbalance over the period from 2003-04. The first item to reference is the two lines on the chart: the LSI line, which is the thinner line, and the closing share price, represented by the thicker line. Recall that the LSI line represents the correlation between volume change and share price change, so there are no volume bars in LSI charts. The scale of the LSI line is measured in dollar value consistent

18

with the share price along the vertical axis. In addition, the LSI line and share price begin at the same fixed point, which represents the closing share price on the start date of the chart. Following a fixed starting point, the LSI line and share price separate, or "**decouple**," based on the development of spikes and overall movement of the LSI line over the one-year or five-year time frame referenced by the chart. Finally, at the top of the chart, the company's name and ticker appear next to the closing price, as well as the share price high (H) and low (L) for the specified time period.

Armed with these important basics we can now take a closer look at LSI charts from the eye of an investor.

The Power of LSI Charts

The LSI line provides a visual history of the supply and demand characteristics of a particular stock. The buying and selling intricacies of the Fidelitys, Putnams and Januses of the investment world, all the way down to small mutual funds, hedge funds, and even individuals, are now "visible" for investors to analyze through spike patterns found along the LSI line. The LSI line provides a unique look into the minds of these investors, revealing much about the institutional sentiment of a given stock. Another way of thinking about LSI charts is a tool that enables the ability to align investment decisions in the same direction as the underlying money flow in a stock. This allows investors to buy those stocks where the institutional environment is positive, and to avoid those stocks or sell short where the environment is negative. Thus, supply and demand is most heavily influenced by those that have the ability to create imbalances, namely institutional investors.

A keen understanding of spike patterns holds the key to unlocking the mystery of underlying institutional forces to make investment decisions. Patterns of spikes are critically important to investors using LSI charts to determine the level of institutional activity and magnitude of an underlying imbalance. Spike patterns also reveal the stage of institutional buying or selling, either early, mid, or late to further assist in the timing of investment decisions.

Investors can assess the probability of future share price movement through spike patterns that reveal the size of an underlying imbalance. As we'll discuss in the chapters ahead, the formation of certain spike patterns result in different probabilities of future share price gains. More conservative spike patterns such as Stair-Steps and Bowls present good historical probabilities of longer-term share price appreciation based on a more stable demand imbalance. However, as we'll see later in this chapter, special spike patterns, known as "power patterns," present not only the highest probability of future share price gains but also reveal some of the most exciting and best performing stocks to be found in the market.

Identifying Basic LSI Chart Patterns

We now turn our attention to a step-by-step look at LSI chart patterns to understand the demand imbalance characteristics associated with some of the market's best performing stocks. Recognizing these key imbalance traits through spike patterns allows investors to gain the insight necessary to gauge future share price behavior. We begin by reviewing the basic set of patterns associated with supply and demand imbalances. As Chapter 1 progresses, we'll review powerful spike patterns that form the building blocks of explosive moves in share price as well as formations associated with turnaround based on imbalance shifts from supply to demand.

Over the charts that follow we'll identify spike patterns and define features that are found in LSI charts. These patterns are characterized by varying levels of supply and demand imbalance. Larger imbalances, as one might expect, strongly correlate to spike activity and produce an upward trajectory of the LSI line. Unique chart features, including ascending deltas, barbs, and positive divergences, are highlighted in bold and defined along with an analysis of the underlying pattern. Understanding and identifying these special patterns and features lead to an entirely new way of discovering the market's leading stock performers.

Investors using LSI charts to make buying and selling decisions require an understanding of the primary investment rules and disciplines outlined in Table 3 — a topic we'll cover in depth in Chapter 2. Among the most important of these is the "1-2" spike combination rule, which is the most fundamental principle investors follow when identifying a demand imbalance and buying a stock. Virtually all patterns described in this section trace their beginnings to an initial 1-2 spike combination. In addition to a spike combination, positive charts must also exhibit an upward trajectory of the LSI line. This upward movement is further confirmation of the presence of a demand imbalance in a given stock. Although negative spikes can occur in a positively oriented LSI chart, a continuous upward trajectory of the LSI line indicates that a demand imbalance is being maintained. Finally, investors make purchases during the formation of **positive divergences**, which are near-term pullbacks or retracements in the share price while the LSI line's trajectory remains positive to neutral. The only exception to this last rule is when the pattern emerges as a Ladder or "V" which we'll illustrate later in the chapter. A keen understanding of these three primary rules is essential for identifying demand imbalances and buying stocks under LSI analysis.

As a final note on the LSI chart examples that are featured in Chapter 1 and in subsequent chapters, we focus primarily on more recent charts throughout the majority of this book although older examples are also used where relevant. This is meant to demonstrate the recurring and consistent nature of key spike patterns that can be found over time, as well as the unique formations that often develop in periods of high market volatility.

Table 3	Three Primary Rules for Buying Stocks Using LSI Charts	
Rule #	**Rule**	**Definition**
1	"1-2" Spike Combination	Primary spike (1) followed by a second, confirmatory spike (2)
2	Upward Line Trajectory	LSI line moving in an ascending trajectory
3	Positive Divergence	Buy into a weakening price versus a positive or neutral LSI line

Spotting Demand Imbalances

A Review of "1-2" Spike Combinations

Virtually all demand imbalances can trace their origins to a "1-2" spike combination — a positive initial spike followed by a second, confirmatory spike resulting in an upward trajectory of the LSI line. These patterns signal the commencement of a demand imbalance and represent a favorable environment for investors to buy or hold a stock. These 1-2 combinations are easy for investors to recognize and are often precipitated by institutional buying in anticipation of a fundamental change in business outlook. Investors using LSI charts may search among thousands of stocks looking specifically for these combinations to find investment opportunities. These patterns can occur in rapid succession, or over the course of a few weeks to months, often serving as the precursor to a Stair-Step or more complex pattern identified later in the chapter.

One-two spike combination patterns appear prominently on the chart as the LSI line begins to decouple, or move upward in advance of the share price. In large capitalization stocks, it is important to recognize a more subtle appearance of these spike combinations due to a higher level of pre-existing institutional ownership. This can cause the LSI line to trail, or lag below the share price on a chart. However, it is important to note from Table 3 that the *trajectory* of the LSI line, not its *position* relative to share price, serves as the critical factor in assessing spike combination patterns. Seasoned LSI investors can often gain an understanding of the existing level of institutional ownership through these varying subtleties of LSI line behavior.

We'll now take a look at an initial series of LSI charts featuring 1-2 spike combinations that demonstrate the emergence of demand imbalances. These combinations correspond to the onset of favorable investing conditions in a stock. Over the charts that follow in this chapter we'll indicate whether a daily LSI chart — typically used to spot imbalances in large, institutionally dominant companies — or a weekly LSI chart is used. We begin with a review of the weekly LSI charts of DGI, AMED and GV (Charts 1-3) that exhibit 1-2 spike combinations resulting in an upward trajectory of the LSI line.

Chart 1–DGI

Out first LSI chart example features DigitalGlobe, a provider of satellite earth mapping services on Chart 1. A 1-2 spike combination is clearly visible in this weekly, five-year chart as spikes 1 and 2 combine to signal the return of institutional buyers into the stock. This initial spike (1) and confirmatory spike (2) result in an upward trajectory of the LSI line to satisfy the first two rules of buying stocks using LSI charts from Table 3. We'll discuss Rule 3 regarding positive divergences in greater detail in Chapter 2. This 1-2 spike pattern signals the initiation of a demand imbalance in DGI shares and a favorable environment for investors. This activity took place as mapping providers came into favor when Google Earth became a must-have application on virtually every desktop computer.

Chart 2–AMED

One-two spike combinations typically occur in lockstep with a shift in the fundamentals of a business or change in outlook. For home health services provider Amedisys, advantageous

Chart 1

DigitalGlobe (DGI) $18.66 H 33.16 L 11.61

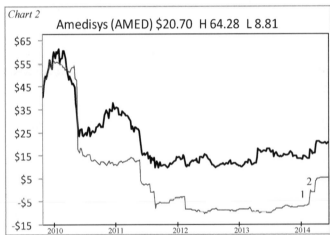

Chart 2

Amedisys (AMED) $20.70 H 64.28 L 8.81

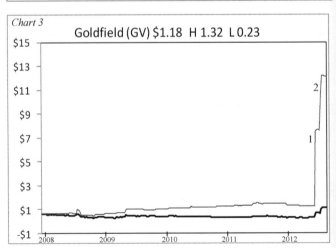

Chart 3

Goldfield (GV) $1.18 H 1.32 L 0.23

conditions returned for investors after a change in management brought institutional investors back into the stock. The 1-2 spike combination in weekly LSI Chart 2 features an initial spike (1) followed one month later by a second, confirmatory spike (2) resulting in the first upward move in LSI line trajectory in almost five years. The demand imbalance that developed reversed a four-year supply imbalance (period of negative LSI line activity from 2010 through 2013) and eventually lifted Amedisys to more than $50 per share in 2015.

Chart 3–GV

Exciting demand imbalance patterns can develop rapidly in very small stocks. Speculative investors would delight in finding this rapid-fire 1-2 spike combination in the weekly, five-year LSI chart of tiny electrical contractor Goldfield. The formation of these patterns in small stocks often precedes positive news or events, in this case the winning of a substantial contract to build a power transmission line located in Texas. The initial spike (1) and confirmatory spike (2) occur almost simultaneously to decouple the LSI line from the share price and signal the emergence of a demand imbalance. Rapidly forming 1-2 combination patterns are more common in smaller stocks and indicate aggressive buying activity and the potential for dramatic investment returns. Following the 1-2 spike combination in this example, Goldfield stock increased to more than $5 per share within twelve months.

Stair-Step Patterns

The signature pattern of LSI charts is called a Stair-Step. No other pattern exemplifies the vivid upward progression of the LSI line as well as the "green light" it represents to investors looking to buy stocks. Whereas the 1-2 spike combination marks the creation of a demand imbalance, a Stair-Step pattern confirms the presence of a demand imbalance through a series of spikes that look like a staircase formed over a sustained period of time. The positive spikes building upon each other create a pattern resembling an ascending flight of stairs with an LSI line that traces an upward trajectory. The magnitude of the spikes usually ranges within the definition of primary spikes in Table 2, and the upward trajectory of the line is fairly consistent throughout the pattern. It should be noted that there is often a lack of any significant negative spikes during the formation, which gives these patterns the distinctive appearance of an upward sequence of steps. For investors, these patterns signify a favorable investing environment in which to enter a stock. The LSI charts of AAPL, ISRG, AMZN (Charts 4-6) to follow are classic examples of Stair-Step patterns over a one-year period that represent an ongoing demand imbalance in their respective shares.

Chart 4–AAPL

Apple's growing popularity among institutional investors following the return of founder Steve Jobs is captured in this Stair-Step pattern on the daily, one-year LSI Chart 4 of Apple from August 2003 to August 2004. Long before consumers had ever heard of an iPhone or iPad, the LSI line reveals institutions jumping back into Apple in anticipation of a return to its glory days of developing innovative new

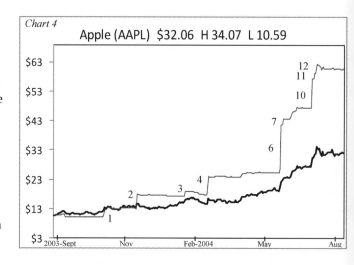

products. The Stair-Step that formed in Apple indicates the creation of a large demand imbalance and continuation of the favorable buying environment in the stock originally signaled by a 1-2 spike combination (spikes 1 and 2). The LSI chart features twelve positive spikes that range in magnitude, including five primary spikes (spikes 1, 2, 4, 6, and 10) and several smaller spikes that serve as markers of heavy institutional buying.

Chart 5–ISRG

Surgical robotics became big business by the turn of the century, led by Intuitive Surgical, maker of the innovative *da Vinci* surgery system. As hospital adoption of *da Vinci* surged during the middle part of the decade, a Stair-Step pattern on this daily, one-year Chart 5 alerted investors to the heavy institutional buying that eventually drove ISRG shares

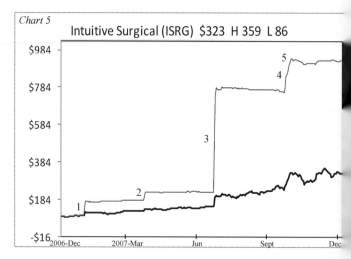

from a low of under $100 to more than $300 by 2007. Four spikes (1, 2, 4, and 5) straddle a major spike (3) on the chart to reveal substantial institutional buying. Spikes 4 and 5 appear to be one spike but are actually two occurring in rapid succession, while the spike at 3 is of such large magnitude that it skews the appearance of the other spikes into looking more like smaller ones. Note the lack of any material institutional selling, or negative spike activity, over this 12-month period that gave investors confidence to maintain positions despite several declines in share price.

Chart 6–AMZN

Following the bursting of the Internet bubble in 2000, shares of the leading Internet companies were shunned by investors and took several years to recover. By mid-decade, however, LSI Chart 6 indicates the return of a favorable buying environment for investors of Amazon before it once again acquired the status of Wall Street darling. A well-formed Stair-Step pattern from

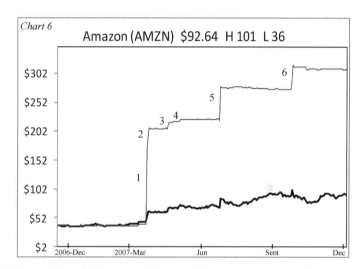

December 2006 to December 2007 was initiated by a rapid 1-2 spike combination (spikes 1 and 2) that signaled the emergence of a demand imbalance in the stock. Notable as well is a bullish decoupling of the LSI line from Amazon's share price following the 1-2 spike combination.

Aggressive Stair-Step Patterns

An aggressive Stair-Step pattern features a steeper ascent of the LSI line and greater density of spikes in comparison to the classic Stair-Steps just highlighted. Aggressive Stair-Steps indicate a more intensive level of institutional buying that corresponds with a major demand imbalance. These patterns provide a highly favorable environment for investors to buy alongside heavy institutional demand. Spikes of many different magnitudes may be present, as primary spikes are often intermingled with major, minor, and micro spikes. The sizable demand imbalances revealed by aggressive Stair-Steps typically result in a stronger and more rapid influence on share price. These patterns are far less uniform than classic Stair-Steps and develop more quickly. The following LSI charts of FSLR, PCLN, TARO, and MDSO (Charts 7 through 10) represent aggressive Stair-Step patterns and signal a highly favorable environment for buyers.

Chart 7–FSLR

For investors that can
withstand added volatility,
aggressive Stair-Step patterns
represent a welcome sign for
buyers on LSI charts. One of
the leading solar plays at the
time of its initial public
offering in late 2006 was First
Solar, a stock widely
considered to be a "must own"
by institutional investors. The
aggressive buying that formed
the Stair-Step in this daily LSI

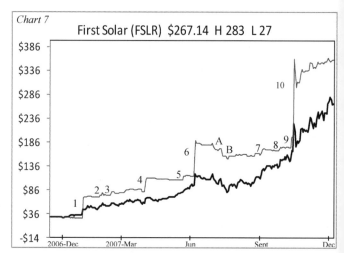

chart of First Solar (Chart 7) features a multitude of spikes in close proximity along a
steeply ascending LSI line. This indicates a more rapidly developing demand imbalance
than found in charts 4 through 6 above and a highly positive environment for investors.
Aggressive Stair-Step patterns often experience short-term periods of negative spike
behavior (negative spikes A and B), but without a material influence on the overall
upward trajectory of the LSI line.

Chart 8-PCLN

One of the most successful
companies of the Internet era
is online travel site, Priceline
(Chart 8). A major demand
imbalance heralded the
emergence of Priceline in 2005,
visible to LSI chartists through
an aggressive Stair-Step
pattern on this weekly chart.
The opportunity for buyers
produced by the aggressive
Stair-Step continued for more
than two years following the

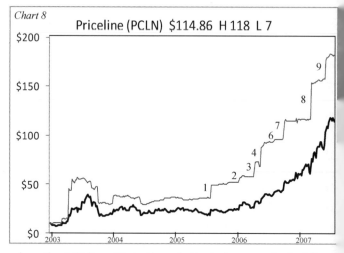

spike at 1 as a series of steps formed on the LSI line. Note the relatively long period of flat
LSI line behavior in the middle portion of the chart, representing a far less favorable
environment for investors, before the spike at 1 indicated a return of institutional buying.

Chart 9–TARO

Institutional investors began snapping up Taro Pharmaceutical shares in 2010 as the small OTC drug developer appeared poised to begin delivering significant increases in revenue and earnings (Chart 9). Following an initial spike at 1, positive conditions for investors continued for a full three and a half years on this weekly chart. What is unique about Taro's aggressive Stair-Step

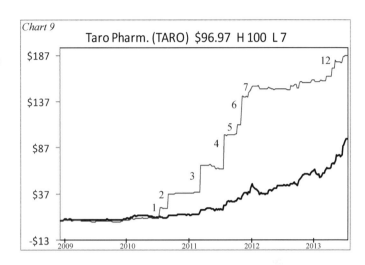

pattern is the increasing trajectory of the LSI line, as spikes occur with greater frequency in the middle-portion of the chart, from spikes 4 through 7. This increasing trajectory indicates a demand imbalance that is growing in intensity and highly favorable for investors.

Chart 10–MDSO

As cloud-based computing became the rage during the first decade of the new century, Medidata Solutions tapped into the cloud for drug developers to access its suite of clinical trial solutions. This weekly, five-year LSI chart (Chart 10) features a particularly aggressive Stair-Step ascending at a steep angle, more resembling a ramp than steps. The feverish pace

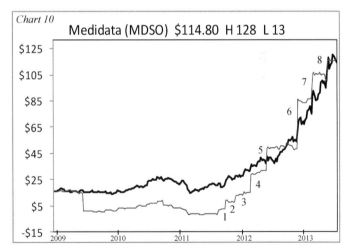

of buying indicated by this pattern provided an opportunity for investors to take advantage alongside the heavy institutional demand. This pattern is highlighted by a series of small spikes (1 through 3) before growing more aggressive as the larger spikes (4 through 8) combined to accentuate the Stair-Step.

Negative Stair-Step Patterns

Stair-Steps can be equally compelling to the downside, as negative patterns indicate an environment that is unfavorable to all investors except those selling short. The striking uniformity of spikes in negative Stair-Step patterns resembles a flight of steps dropping downward. These patterns reflect large supply imbalances created by heavy institutional selling over time. Negative Stair-Steps can be of the more classic variety, with a consistent downward trajectory of the LSI line, or aggressive when associated with a spike-rich, steep downward decline. The LSI charts of COH, IBM, CMG, and ASH (Charts 11 through 14) represent a classic variety of negative Stair-Step patterns that signal a warning to investors.

Chart 11–COH

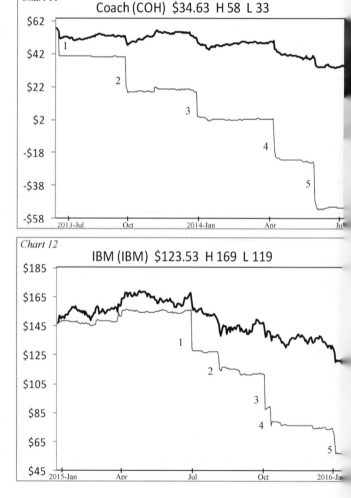

By the summer of 2013, upscale hand bag maker Coach began to fall out of favor among the fashion conscious. This exceptionally well formed example of a negative Stair-Step pattern indicates the mass exodus of institutional investors as stiff competition from Kate Spade and Michael Kors began to take a toll on Coach. Chart 11 flashes a clear warning to investors of a large supply imbalance.

Chart 12-IBM

Berkshire Hathway's foray into the tech sector began to sour in 2015 as a major supply imbalance developed in the shares of mighty IBM, starting with the negative spike at 1. A negative Stair-Step builds with additional spikes (2 through 5) pressuring IBM shares to new lows by early 2016.

Chart 13–CMG

Despite its status as of one of the hottest new concepts in FreshMex, investors would have been wise to take notice of a sizable supply imbalance that developed in Chipotle during the early months of 2008. As growing pains from its rapid expansion began to emerge at the company, the daily LSI chart (13) of CMG suffers a series of negative spikes throughout the year. A negative Stair-Step pattern

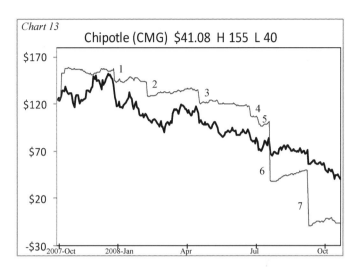

forms through a series of smaller spikes (1 through 5) before increasing in downward intensity with negative primary spikes at 6 and 7. The major supply imbalance is nearly continuous throughout the first two-thirds of the chart before it grew in magnitude following spike 6.

Chart 14–ASH

The 2008 Financial Crisis was particularly harsh to companies in cyclical industries, including specialty chemical maker Ashland. As sales began to falter, a large supply imbalance formed in Ashland shares following the negative spike at 1 on daily Chart 14, which served as an initial cautionary note to investors. Following the negative spike at 1 a series of additional spikes occurred to

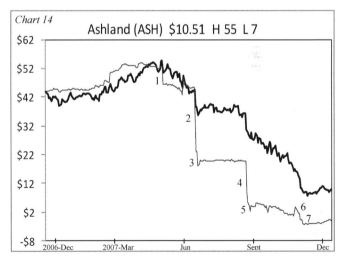

create a negative Stair-Step pattern (spikes 1 through 6). This daily, one-year chart lacks the uniformity of negative spikes in Coach, but the downward trajectory of the LSI line is unmistakable in revealing heavy institutional selling in Ashland shares.

29

Aggressive Negative Stair-Step Patterns

Negative Stair-Steps that are of a more aggressive nature feature a steeper descent of the LSI line and a greater density of negative spikes in comparison to the classic variety of negative Stair-Step patterns just highlighted. These patterns provide a more immediate warning to investors by revealing stocks with material supply imbalances due to major institutional selling. These supply imbalances are visible on the LSI line through varying combinations of spike magnitudes. The following LSI charts of VRX, BC, AIG, GEOS, and IMH (Charts 15 through 19) highlight aggressive negative Stair-Steps formed by heavy institutional selling.

Chart 15–VRX

Even the best efforts of hedge fund luminary Bill Ackman were not enough to override a massive supply imbalance in shares of Valeant in late 2015. Despite purchases of roughly one million shares in the fourth quarter of 2015, an aggressive negative Stair-Step ultimately dictated the course of Valeant following a steep plunge in the LSI line (spikes 3 through 7).

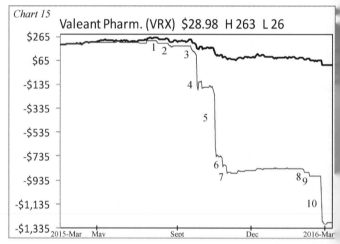

Chart 16–BC

Sales of recreational boats ran aground in 2005 as consumers began to rein in the largest excesses of their home equity withdrawals. LSI Chart 16 of leading boat maker Brunswick, whose popular brands include Sea Ray and Bayliner, exhibits a steep decent of the LSI line alerting investors to the presence of a major supply imbalance in the stock.

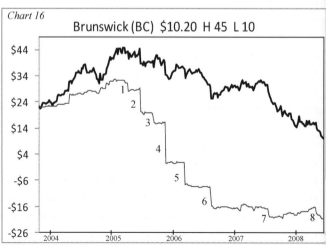

30

Chart 17–AIG

One of the more notorious stocks of the 2008 market meltdown that became a favored target of regulators was insurer AIG. Weekly, five-year LSI Chart 17 highlights the massive liquidation that took place as institutional investors hit the sell button on the stock. This pattern can actually trace its beginnings to 2005 with the large negative spikes at 1 and 2, flashing an early warning to

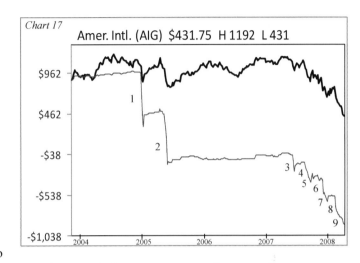

AIG investors. As the Financial Crisis deepened, the negative Stair-Step pattern turns aggressive, beginning with the minor spike at 3. Following this spike, the LSI line plunges, reflecting the heavy degree of selling that set in upon AIG. *Note an adjusted share price for a reverse stock split in 2012.

Chart 18–GEOS

The 2015 plunge in crude oil prices led to a number of casualties in the oil sector, among them seismic oil exploration company Geospace (Chart 18). As revenue and earnings sank so too did Geospace shares, in a particularly vivid, spike-rich aggressive negative Stair-Step. This pattern is striking in that it features twelve minor and micro spikes over just a two year period forcing a 90

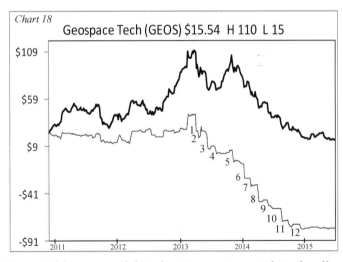

percent plunge in the stock. Another notable aspect of this chart is an attempted stock rally in late 2013 that eventually fizzled as the steeply descending LSI line indicated institutional investors were actually the ones selling.

Chart 19–IMH

Investors may have known something was terribly wrong with home loan originator Impac Mortgage when three share price peaks (A, B, and C) at the beginning of this chart were offset by a diverging LSI line. This weekly, five-year LSI chart (19) of IMH from 2004-08 provides a short seller's dream scenario. A victim of the housing market crash, Impac's rather extraordinary

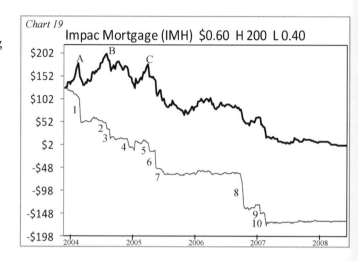

Chart 19
Impac Mortgage (IMH) $0.60 H 200 L 0.40

LSI chart pattern reveals a massive supply imbalance that pressured its shares from a high of $200 to under $1 over the ensuing five year period. The aggressive negative Stair-Step pattern traced its roots to early 2004, well before the housing market hit the skids, and comprised ten negative spikes. The three share price peaks at A, B, and C, juxtaposed against a negative LSI line, are called **negative divergences** and provide opportunities for short sellers under LSI analysis. These formations will be covered in greater detail in Chapter 2.

Concluding our review of basic "1-2" and Stair-Step spike patterns, we have analyzed LSI charts featuring supply and demand imbalances that have been fairly uniform in appearance. We now review more complex and exciting patterns formed by even larger demand imbalances.

LSI Power Patterns: Wings, Ladders and Waves

Massive, emerging demand imbalances, particularly in stocks with little or no existing institutional ownership, result in dramatic LSI chart patterns. These patterns are highly coveted by LSI chartists and associated with the biggest and most explosive stock gainers in the market. While the 1-2 spike combination remains at the heart of virtually all LSI patterns, power patterns are typically associated with a much more aggressive and complex series of spike patterns. These patterns are notable for a rapid succession of spikes across a range of different magnitudes. LSI power patterns are known as Wings, Ladders, and Waves, and many of the market's best performing stocks can trace their emergence to one of these three patterns.

Wing Patterns

Among LSI power patterns, Wings are one of most distinctive formations that can result in significant share price gains. Wings are unique by virtue of a major initial spike that launches the LSI line from the share price in a sudden, vertical trajectory. Then, over time, the gap between the LSI line and underlying share price widens, forming a pattern resembling a bird's wing. Wings represent the onset of institutional buying that either reverses a negative trend or, more commonly, follows a long period of inactivity to signal the onset of a favorable buying environment. The major spike, called a "Wing spike," indicates a surge in demand often prompted by a material change in the fundamental outlook of the company's business. As the Wing forms, additional positive spikes occur, contributing to the development of the pattern. Another LSI feature prominent in Wing patterns is an **ascending delta**. Ascending deltas are characterized by an LSI line that rises at a steeper slope than the share price. Ascending deltas are highly positive patterns that appear to "lift" the share price higher over time. From a supply and demand perspective, ascending deltas indicate heavy institutional demand working through an ample supply of stock. An increase in share price eventually arrives when the large existing supply of shares is exhausted. By definition, a Wing pattern features a major spike followed by an upward trajectory of the LSI line to create an ascending delta.

Chart 20–APSG

Following the events of 9/11, the U.S. Government dramatically stepped up its intelligence capabilities to include the enhanced monitoring of cellular transmissions with solutions provided by Applied Signal. The abrupt nature by which APSG shares came into favor led to the formation of a Wing pattern on weekly, five-year Chart 20, beginning with a

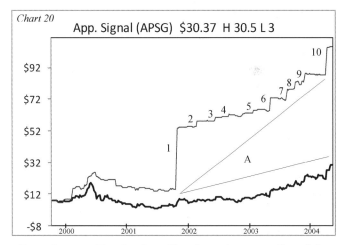

major spike at 1 (Wing spike) signaling a burst of institutional buying. An ascending delta (A) begins to build in the months following the appearance of the Wing spike, driven by several smaller spikes (2 through 9). The faster ascent of the LSI line versus the share price that forms the ascending delta (A) reveals the presence of a large supply overhang that required almost one year to work through before the share price rose rapidly in 2003.

Chart 21–ARII

Shares of boxcar manufacturer American Railcar snapped back into favor during the rebound in transportation stocks after the Financial Crisis. What is distinctive about this Wing pattern in the weekly LSI chart of ARII (Chart 21-A) is the number of small (micro) spikes present, following the primary Wing spike at 2. The unique aspect of micro spike patterns are the

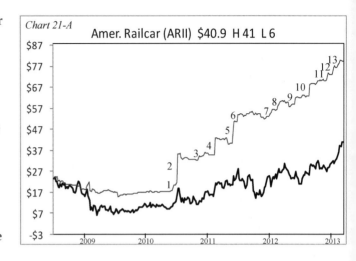

Chart 21-A
Amer. Railcar (ARII) $40.9 H 41 L 6

multitude of spikes that are typically associated with these formations (a total of 13 in this example). This represents a period of near continuous institutional buying in the stock. The spikes that occurred in this example developed over the course of two and half years indicating a significant ongoing demand imbalance.

LSI Chart 21-B is the same chart represented in 21-A for the purpose of highlighting the ascending delta (A) formation, which confirms the Wing pattern, as well as several positive divergences (W through Z). Positive divergences are buying opportunities under LSI analysis that form when the share price declines against a neutral or rising LSI line, which we'll cover in detail in

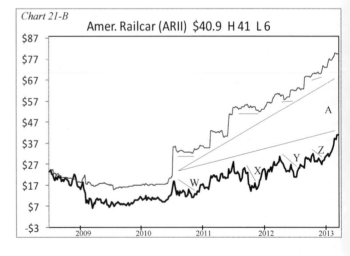

Chart 21-B
Amer. Railcar (ARII) $40.9 H 41 L 6

Chapter 2. Similar to the ascending delta visible in LSI Chart 20 of Applied Signal, the area between the two lines of the ascending delta continues to grow before the share price eventually closes the gap. We begin to see this gap close at the latter stages of Chart 21-B with the ascent in share price (dark line) that is visible just below the "A" designated on the chart.

Chart 22–GLOG

Our final Wing example is a fast moving pattern on the weekly LSI chart of GasLog (Chart 22), an operator of liquefied natural gas (LNG) tankers during the height of the gas confrontation between Russia and Ukraine in 2014. The major Wing spike at 1, closely followed by spikes 2 through 4, indicates a rapidly building demand imbalance in the stock. An ascending delta

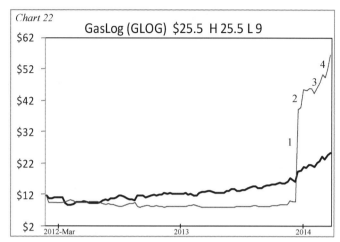

Chart 22 GasLog (GLOG) $25.5 H 25.5 L 9

formed between the LSI line and share price highlighting significant institutional activity.

Ladder Patterns

Ladders are among the most dramatic and sought after of LSI power patterns. These formations result from a sudden, aggressive burst of spikes, unlike the more drawn out development of spikes in Wing patterns. A Ladder forms when multiple spikes occur in quick succession, one right after the other, to produce an upward thrust in the LSI line. Most Ladders see a near vertical rise in the LSI line, while others may display a compounding of small spikes. These patterns are associated with Stair-Steps, but develop so rapidly that they more closely resemble the upward rungs of a ladder. A Ladder has been described as a Stair-Step on steroids, and after reviewing many examples it is hard to argue with that comparison. The most exciting aspects of these patterns are the eye-catching surge of the LSI line and their immediate and, oftentimes, dramatic impact on share price. The formation of a Ladder pattern is considered a most prized discovery for LSI chartists.

From a supply and demand perspective, the formation of a Ladder represents a massive demand imbalance, often against a relatively small supply of shares. These patterns usually occur in smaller stocks with little existing institutional ownership. By the time a Ladder formation is complete — over the course of several weeks to months — institutional ownership has been known to increase from less than 5 percent of total shares outstanding to as high as 40 percent in some cases. Ladder formations revealing massive demand imbalances have signaled the emergence of such iconic brands as Deckers Outdoor (UGG boots), Monster Beverage, and Keurig Green Mountain.

Chart 23–BJRI

A prime example of the near vertical LSI line ascent that can be found in Ladders occurred in 2002 in the weekly, five-year chart of fast growing pizza chain, BJ's Restaurants. The Ladder in LSI Chart 23 corresponds to a massive demand imbalance that developed in the stock as institutional ownership rose from less than 15 percent of total shares outstanding to

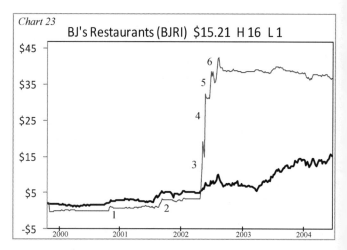

more than 35 percent over a compressed period of just six months. The LSI line reveals how quickly Ladders can develop, as exhibited by consecutive spikes (3 through 6) and the highly favorable environment for investors that they signify. That is because before a Ladder forms, a demand imbalance is usually in place, as seen here with the small spikes at 1 and 2. The LSI chart of BJ's represents a classic Ladder pattern.

Chart 24–DECK

One of the most iconic brands in fashion footwear to emerge at the turn of the century was the UGG Boot, marketed by a small company called Deckers. As UGG emerged, so too did Deckers — from an institutionally neglected company into a must-own stock. Against this backdrop, Deckers' weekly, five-year LSI chart (24) develops into a Ladder pattern (spikes 6

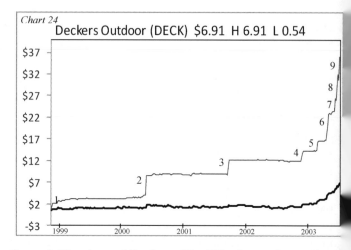

through 9) beginning with the spike at 6. The chart of Deckers, like BJ's above, shows that most Ladders develop in stocks already experiencing a demand imbalance, represented here by spikes 1 through 5. The Ladder that developed in Deckers resulted in the steady rise of its share price, eventually climbing to more than $100 in 2014.

Chart 25–EPIC

A rather unique Ladder formed in the weekly LSI Chart 25 of software solutions provider EPIC, in 2003. In this example, we find a Ladder consisting solely of micro and minor spikes (2 through 9), with the pattern spanning almost an entire year. Unlike the previous two examples, the Ladder in EPIC developed without warning from a multiyear equilibrium of supply and demand. The

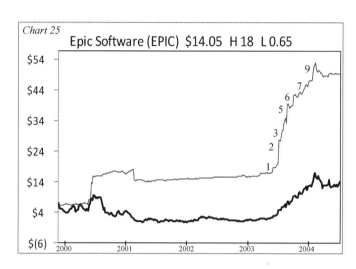

Chart 25
Epic Software (EPIC) $14.05 H 18 L 0.65

major demand imbalance that produced the Ladder of EPIC indicated an immediate opportunity for investors that led to a tenfold increase in share price in the year following its formation.

Wave Patterns

LSI Waves are an explosive power pattern that feature rather odd but highly positive spike behavior. Wave patterns acquire their name from a condensed period of rapid up-and-down spike activity that looks similar to the wave pattern of a seismograph during an earthquake. A Wave is a series of two or more upward and downward spikes occurring over a short duration. Each subsequent downward spike, however, is usually of lesser magnitude than the preceding positive spike, so that despite the upward and downward movement, the LSI line's overall trajectory remains upward. The pattern is interesting by virtue of having just as many negative spikes as positive ones. Yet, despite this seeming contradiction in the supply and demand trend, Waves boast a remarkable track record of signaling significant share price appreciation. Wave patterns are unfortunately rare, occurring in only a handful of stocks annually, but have been shown on average to produce a doubling or more in share price over the ensuing twelve- to fifteen-month period. While the underlying cause of this pattern from a supply and demand perspective is not well understood, the distinctiveness of a Wave pattern makes it among the most recognizable on LSI charts. The LSI charts of CLFD, PATK, HCI, and MNST (Charts 26 through 29) represent a diverse collection of Waves to reveal the highly unique nature of this power pattern.

Chart 26–CLFD

The odd but explosive nature of Wave patterns is captured vividly in the weekly LSI chart (26) of communications equipment maker Clearfield. Institutional investors surged into the stock in 2013 when it was rumored that Google's initiative to bring gigabit speed optical fiber to the home would include Clearfield products. The Wave pattern in this example develops

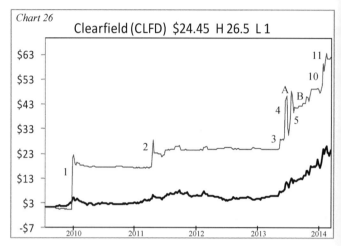

abruptly following a spike at 3 and is created by positive spikes 4 and 5, and negative spikes A and B. While these negative spikes may lead to the conclusion that the demand imbalance has evaporated, the pattern's sheer volatility indicates that something unusually bullish is under way. Following the completion of the Wave, we find a string of positive spikes (6 through 11), pulling Clearfield shares higher.

Chart 27–PATK

A particularly violent Wave forms in the pattern rich weekly LSI chart (27) of manufactured home and RV firm Patrick Industries. Investors began to aggressively take positions in the stock on the anticipation of sharply higher earnings that followed a string of acquisitions. Patrick's earnings didn't disappoint, and a large demand imbalance was already under way as indicated by a small Ladder

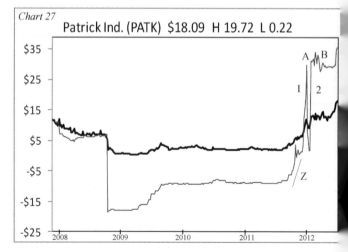

pattern (Z) that formed a couple of months prior to the Wave. The Wave in this example is made up of two positive spikes at 1 and 2, and a large negative spike at A. Another interesting facet of this unique LSI chart comes with what appears to be a second Wave pattern consisting of only small (micro) spikes at B. This example of Patrick provides one of the most remarkable collections of LSI power patterns packed onto one chart we've ever encountered, reflecting the sheer magnitude of the demand imbalance that developed in the stock.

Chart 28–HCI

A rather unusual cross between a Wave and a Ladder pattern developed in the weekly LSI chart (28) of HCI in 2012. The pattern formed as the Florida-based home insurer completed a major acquisition that institutional investors were speculating would boost earnings. The pattern in HCI comprising spikes 1 through 5 is either a Ladder with **Barbs** or a Wave

Chart 28

HCI Group (HCI) $42.24 H 42 L 4

with much smaller down waves. A Barb is a small negative spike that immediately follows a major or primary positive spike, and is associated with highly bullish patterns discussed more extensively in Chapter 2. Both characteristics indicate a massive demand imbalance created by institutional buying that resulted in a highly favorable environment for investors.

Chart 29–MNST

An explosive LSI pattern is found on the weekly chart (29) of Monster Beverage during the period that marked the company's emergence on Wall Street. Monster Beverage rose from obscurity in 2002, as the company transformed its business from Hansen's sodas into energy drinks that would eventually rival incumbent Red Bull. The LSI chart of

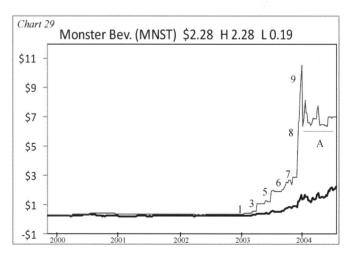

Chart 29

Monster Bev. (MNST) $2.28 H 2.28 L 0.19

Monster reveals the formation of a massive demand imbalance created by institutional investors rapidly taking positions in a stock where there had been little previous fund ownership. The pattern begins with a highly bullish decoupling of the LSI line from the share price followed by a spike rich Stair-Step (spikes 1 through 7) and associated ascending delta. The major spike visible after spike 7 is actually made up of two spikes, 8 and 9. An oddity of the pattern forms above the line (A), which shows a muted Wave pattern followed by positive and negative spikes. The LSI chart of Monster provides a spectacular example of what highly aggressive institutional buying looks like in a small, previously neglected stock.

LSI Turnaround Patterns: Bowl, U and V Patterns

LSI charts can be a powerful tool when looking for stocks poised for a turnaround. Our review now focuses on spike patterns associated specifically with turnaround stocks as the LSI line trajectory shifts from negative to positive. This reversal is driven by dissipation of a supply imbalance and a shift toward a demand imbalance. The three turnaround patterns featured in this section are defined by the magnitude of the underlying imbalance and speed of the associated share price turnaround. LSI Bowl patterns are the slowest moving and typically occur in larger market capitalization stocks. LSI "U" patterns signal an abrupt shift from negative to positive, and "V" patterns can occur somewhat violently with an instantaneous shift in imbalance from supply to demand. The characteristic these patterns all share is a reversal in direction of the LSI line that results in the return of a favorable environment for investors. These patterns often mark an absolute bottom in the stock and are powerful indicators of a return to a sustained period of positive share price activity.

Bowl Patterns

Bowls are the slowest developing of LSI turnaround patterns. As their name implies, Bowls feature rounded LSI lines as the trajectory of the line gradually shifts from negative to positive. Bowls tend to occur in larger market cap stocks, often in cyclical industries, as significant institutional demand is usually needed to reverse the large supply imbalance previously in place. These turnaround patterns are distinctive in appearance and highly effective in providing an opportunity for investors to "bottom pick" stocks. Bowls are completed by satisfying the 1-2 spike combination rules that create a buying opportunity during a positive divergence (see Table 3). The following LSI charts of AMAT and WBMD (Charts 30 and 31) feature examples of Bowl patterns that represented turnaround opportunities for investors.

Chart 30–AMAT

Semiconductor equipment maker Applied Materials operates in the highly cyclical computer chip industry. As a new leg upward in the chip market began in 2013, the weekly LSI chart (30) of AMAT features a Bowl pattern highlighting a shift from a slight negative bias of the LSI line into a positive trend. Bowls typically take place in larger market cap

stocks, such as AMAT, and tend to develop slowly and build momentum. There are two micro spikes at 1 and 2 that indicate the formation of a small demand imbalance, before the primary spike at 3 provides confirmation of a positive environment for investors. The continuing development of spikes (4 through 7) accentuates the Bowl pattern traced by the curve (A) and affirms a demand imbalance in the stock.

Chart 31–WBMD

A rebound in web advertising revenue in 2013 at leading health information portal WebMD brought institutional investors back to its attractively priced shares leading to the formation of a Bowl pattern. The Bowl that developed in this weekly LSI chart (31) is much more uniform than that of AMAT above and, as we'll see in Chapter 2, often very similar

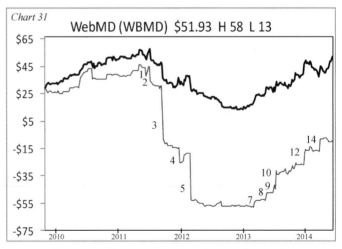

to the U patterns that we'll discuss next. The steep descent of the spikes (1 through 6) resembles a negative Ladder, before small spikes at 7 and 8 indicate the initial stages of a shift from supply to demand imbalance. The progression of positive spikes from 9 through 14 builds upon the appearance of a Bowl and confirms a growing demand imbalance.

U Patterns

U Patterns represent a more abrupt shift in imbalance from supply to demand in comparison to the Bowl patterns featured above. These turnaround patterns display a positive spike after a period of relatively flat LSI line movement that occurs following a negative spike. What is notable about this pattern is that both the negative and positive spikes in the formation are of roughly similar magnitudes to create their resemblance to the letter "U ." These patterns indicate a cessation of an existing supply imbalance created by institutional sellers and the emergence of a demand imbalance in the stock following the completion (positive) spike that forms the U. The creation of a U pattern following a positive spike also represents a shift in LSI line trajectory from negative to positive. The following LSI chart examples of AOL, MDCO, and DAN (Charts 32 through 34) represent U pattern stocks that highlight a shift from supply to demand imbalance and the unique symmetry of this formation.

Chart 32–AOL

Distinction in U patterns originates from their symmetry, as we find in the weekly LSI chart (32) of Internet portal pioneer AOL. The shares of AOL, formerly known as America Online, were largely without interest for almost two years following their spin-off from parent Time Warner in 2009. Experienced investors will recognize the phenomena of post spin-off institutional

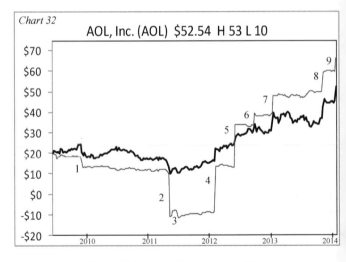

selling as holders of the parent company typically sell the smaller (spun-off) company because it doesn't meet the defined investment criteria of the fund. This institutional trait is evident in AOL with the two negative spikes (1 and 2) that took place after the company separated from Time Warner. A U pattern is formed in this example with the positive spike (4) offsetting the negative primary spike (2) as the imbalance pattern shifts from supply to demand. A small negative spike (3) is noted but does not influence the U formation in this example. Highlighting the return of a demand imbalance in AOL shares are additional positive spikes (5 through 9) that combine over the course of two years to produce a Stair-Step pattern.

Chart 33–MDCO

As sales rebounded for a key company drug, the weekly LSI chart (33) of The Medicines formed a distinctive U pattern in early 2010. Spikes 1 and 2 on this weekly LSI chart complete a rather short duration U pattern, confirming a change from supply to demand imbalance in the stock. While it took several months following the U for the arrival of positive spikes at 3 and 4, a reversal in

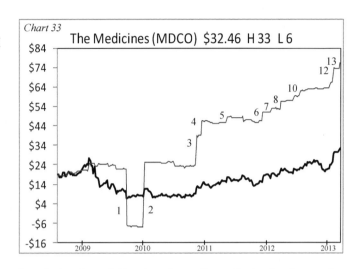

the trajectory of the LSI line was already in place following the spike at 2. As the demand imbalance grows we find a rich pattern of small spikes (5 through 13) occurring as sales for the company continued to strengthen.

Chart 34–DAN

Near death experiences for companies can produce dramatic changes in supply and demand imbalance patterns. None was more interesting to speculative investors than weekly LSI Chart 34 of highly leveraged auto parts maker Dana during the height of the Financial Crisis. A bucket-like U is formed by the combination of negative spikes (2 through 3)

and a positive spike (4). This chart is also unique by virtue of the U pattern triggering a Ladder formation (5 through 9). This U pattern highlights how quickly a heavy supply imbalance can shift to a major demand imbalance, in this case driven by fears over an impending bankruptcy that failed to materialize.

V Patterns

V patterns are much more rapid and actionable LSI turnaround formations, in contrast with the U and Bowl patterns just described. The V pattern marks an instantaneous change in LSI line trajectory, usually developing in conjunction with small (micro) spikes as opposed to the larger spikes found in U patterns. V patterns completely bypass the supply and demand equilibrium stage to look just like the letter of the alphabet they resemble. And unlike U and Bowl turnaround patterns, V's represent an immediate buying opportunity for investors following the positive spikes that form to complete the pattern. V patterns typically arise during extreme market conditions or corporate events that precipitate immediate shifts in institutional sentiment. The following examples of Franklin Resources and FedEx (Charts 35 and 36) represent V pattern turnaround formations that took place during the height of market volatility in early 2009 following the Financial Crisis.

Chart 35–BEN

A classic V pattern takes place on the daily, one-year LSI chart (35) of investment management giant Franklin Resources in early 2009. The multitude of negative spikes leading into the V pattern underscores the major supply imbalance that was pressuring the stock during the height of the Financial Crisis. The V pattern is created as the negative spike at 2 is reversed by a positive spike at 3, accentuated by

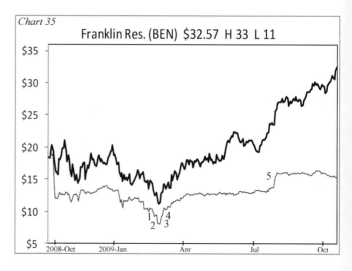

spikes 1 and 4. This pattern indicates an instantaneous reversal of supply imbalance to demand imbalance and the return of a more favorable investing environment in BEN, in this case led by institutional investors betting on a rebound in equity values. Note the multitude of small negative spikes that preceded the negative spike at 1, highlighting the significant degree of institutional selling prior to formation of the V pattern. After completion of the V, we see an uptrend in the trajectory of the LSI line boosted by the positive spike at 5, followed by a substantial turnaround in Franklin shares.

Chart 36–FDX

As investors began to realize the world wasn't coming to an end during the Financial Crisis, buyers came rushing back into the largest global companies, including FedEx (Chart 36). This rapid sentiment change from negative to positive led to the formation of a V pattern produced by a minor negative spike at 2 and three small spikes upward (3 through 5). Although V pattern

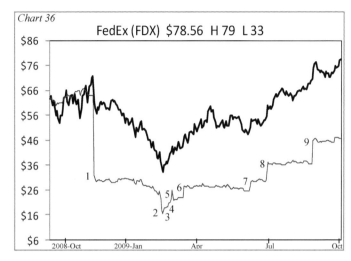

turnarounds are a rarity among LSI charts, they represent an immediate and powerful shift to a demand imbalance, making them a much sought after pattern by LSI chartists.

Conclusion

LSI charts reveal the secretive and hidden influences on supply and demand created by institutional investors, empowering LSI investors with an entirely new way of discovering investment opportunities. Understanding the differing spike patterns formed by supply and demand imbalances that we've covered in this chapter provides an opportunity to find stocks in advance of significant price moves. Investors can now identify the most favorable environment in which to buy and sell stocks. Conservative investors may prefer using straightforward patterns, such as "1-2" spike combinations, Stair Steps, and turnaround Bowl and U patterns. More speculative investors can take advantage of Wings, Ladders, and Waves to discover massive demand imbalances that propel the next big winners in the market. Armed with an understanding of these patterns and the basic rules of LSI investing we'll put this knowledge to work in Chapter 2 and explore how to buy stocks using LSI charts.

Chapter 2

Buying Stocks Using LSI Charts

In this chapter we explore the basics of buying stocks using LSI charts. Taking all we have learned from Chapter 1, including the influence of supply and demand imbalances upon future share price movement and the ability to identify key LSI patterns, we can now review the process of buying stocks using LSI charts. Chapter 2 provides a step-by-step guide of the buying decision process through the identification of spike patterns, describing them from an investor's perspective to locate specific buy points as they develop on an LSI chart.

We begin with a look at the most basic of buy patterns, the "1-2" spike combination, to illustrate each of the primary rules outlined in Table 3 that govern buying decisions under LSI analysis. As the chapter unfolds, we'll review patterns with an increasing level of complexity to build on our understanding of buying decisions using LSI. Following an opening discussion of 1-2 spike combinations using a single LSI chart, we'll then review patterns using a sequence of three LSI charts for each example. These charts are included to represent the period *before* a buying opportunity develops, *during*, as the buying opportunity unfolds, and *after* the buying opportunity has matured. Each sequence of charts includes an "LSI Analysis" discussion correlating the specific pattern to buy points, as well as the appropriate investment action to take. We revisit a handful of examples whose patterns were originally outlined in Chapter 1 to gain insight into the imbalance trends that formed leading up to the creation of a buy signal.

Each example indicates whether a daily, one-year LSI chart or a weekly, five-year chart is used. As discussed in Chapter 1, large capitalization stocks, such as those of the S&P 500 and Dow Jones Industrial Average, usually feature a large percentage of the total shares outstanding in the hands of institutional investors, which makes buying decisions best identified using more sensitive daily LSI charts. Smaller capitalization stocks typically experience dramatic changes in institutional ownership, making the LSI patterns more pronounced on weekly, five-year LSI charts. As we'll discuss in Chapter 3 through a review of specific case studies, advanced investors often incorporate a combination of daily and weekly LSI charts into their strategies to optimize performance according to particular disciplines. For the purposes of clarity and understanding, we will focus our review of buying decisions in this chapter on daily charts for large capitalization stocks and weekly charts for all other stocks, unless otherwise indicated.

In Chapter 2 we discuss the importance of the underlying size of a demand imbalance as determined by chart patterns. LSI charts patterns can also be used to indicate the magnitude of an imbalance, which correspond directly with the degree of institutional buying. Key patterns dictate whether it's advisable to purchase a stock immediately, or to await a near-term pullback in share price. We will introduce unique LSI formations, such as **positive divergences, ascending deltas**, and **barbs** that allow investors to optimize buying decisions.

Using "1-2" Spike Combinations to Make Investment Decisions

The "1-2" spike combination is the most fundamental of those used to make investment decisions using LSI charts. It serves as the basis for buy signals and is visible even in some of the most complex patterns covered later in this chapter. As outlined in Table 3 of Chapter 1, the 1-2 spike combination consists of an initial (primary) spike followed closely by a second (confirmatory) spike. This 1-2 pattern also results in an upward trajectory of the LSI line and is often the precursor to Stair-Step and aggressive Stair-Step patterns. The 1-2 combination is rather simple to identify and indicates the formation of a demand imbalance. The LSI charts featured in examples 37 through 42 highlight 1-2 spike combinations among both large and small cap stocks that result in the creation of a buy signal.

Chart 37—F

It is often hard to imagine that Ford shares plunged all the way down to one dollar during the depths of the Financial Crisis in 2008, until recalling General Motors actually went bankrupt over this period. As the dust began to settle in early 2009, institutional investors can be "seen" regaining enough confidence to climb back into Ford stock in LSI Chart 37.

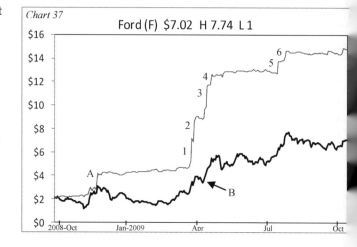

Chart 37

Ford (F) $7.02 H 7.74 L 1

Investors would note a solitary spike (A) indicating that an imbalance shift from negative to positive may have already been under way before a 1-2 spike combination forms with a quick succession of spikes (1 and 2). A buy signal in Ford is confirmed by the upward trajectory of the LSI line leading investors to purchase Ford shares into the first positive divergence (share price decline at B) immediately following the 1-2 combination. Positive divergence patterns present buying opportunities as the share price weakens against a positive or flat LSI line.

Chart 38—GCI

Another survivor of the Financial Crisis, remarkably, was *USA Today* publisher Gannett. Newspaper publishers had already been in a steady decline before 2008, losing market share to Internet rivals. But LSI Chart 38 shows a reversal pattern in Gannett as the highly negative LSI line trajectory begins to shift positive following a 1-2 spike combination (spikes 1 and 2).

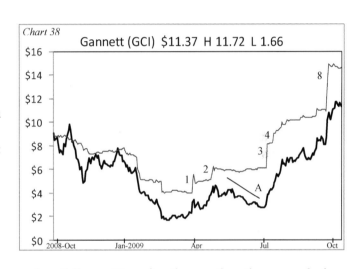

Chart 38

Gannett (GCI) $11.37 H 11.72 L 1.66

While the LSI line trajectory turns only mildly positive after these spikes, the reversal of the negative pattern is relevant nonetheless in signaling a change in institutional sentiment. Investors looking to purchase Gannett shares would await a positive divergence formation following the 1-2 combination which occurs during the relatively long pullback at trend line A.

Chart 39—BSX

Given up largely for dead following its disastrous acquisition of Guidant in 2006, Chart 39 indicates that heart stent maker Boston Scientific finally began to find interest among institutional investors in late 2013. The first half of this weekly, five-year LSI chart

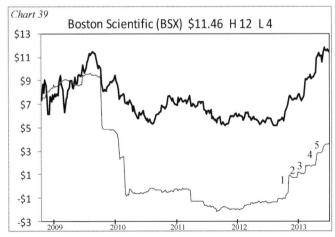

Chart 39

Boston Scientific (BSX) $11.46 H 12 L 4

shows a heavy supply imbalance continuing over the course of almost three years, as indicated by several negative spikes. The turn for BSX came swiftly with a 1-2 spike combination that was reinforced in rapid succession by three additional spikes (3 through 5). The upward trajectory of the LSI line produced by these spikes confirms a buy signal following spike 2.

Chart 40—EBAY

Online auctioneer eBay's long decline that began in 2005 from a high of $50 culminated with an eight-year low in share price by March of 2009. Mired in a period of higher spending to build infrastructure, institutional investors had long since soured on eBay due to lower earnings. In 2009, Chart 40 indicates that eBay began to rebound in earnest following a 1-2 spike combination (spikes 1

and 2). Although the magnitude of the first spike is small, the larger spike at 2 confirms the pattern and causes an upward jump in the LSI line. Spikes at 3 and 4 further confirm institutional buying taking place. Investors would purchase eBay during the first positive divergence following the initial 1-2 combination.

Chart 41—MGAM

The emergence of institutional buying in MGAM shares as signaled by spikes 1 and 2 in Chart 41 came after four years of flat LSI line behavior. Multimedia Games carved out a strong niche by providing slot gaming to the Native American casino market, but had suffered from a deep slump in the aftermath of the Financial Crisis. The 1-2 spike

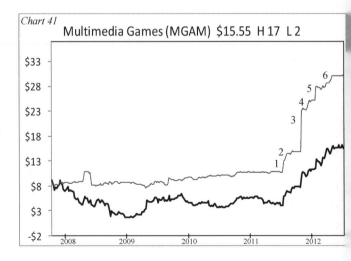

pattern forms in rapid succession in this weekly, five-year chart to produce a rise in the LSI line and confirm a buy signal. The multitude of spikes that follow the 1-2 combination indicate a strong demand imbalance under way that resulted in a significant rise in share price over the next 12 months.

Chart 42—ENV

Following its IPO in 2010, Envestnet rode a broad upswing in the stock market as a provider of wealth management solutions to financial advisors. The LSI chart of ENV (Chart 42) is an exciting example of a 1-2 spike combination serving as the beginning stages of a more powerful formation, in this case a Ladder. Although the Ladder in this example forms after the spike at 3, the 1-2 combination has already generated a buy signal into the first positive divergence following spike 2. The steep ascent of the LSI line produced by spikes 3 through 6 leads to a significant increase in share price, demonstrating the power of major demand imbalances.

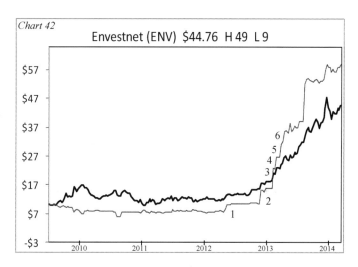

Chart 42

Envestnet (ENV) $44.76 H 49 L 9

Identifying Buy Signals

Identifying key LSI patterns as they emerge is essential to buying stocks ahead of potentially significant share price moves. Over the following examples, we will feature a sequence of three LSI charts covering periods "before" (chart-A), "during" (chart-B) and, "after" (chart-C) the emergence of a buy signal. The "before" chart demonstrates that major demand imbalances can often begin in stocks experiencing little or no institutional activity. As a demand imbalance develops, the "during" chart identifies the LSI pattern that results in a buy signal and includes an "LSI Analysis" review discussion. The chart sequence is complete with an "after" chart that provides a look at the period following a buy signal to reveal the strong influence demand imbalances can have on future share price behavior. These examples begin with a review of the basic patterns found in daily LSI charts of larger stocks, before moving to more complex patterns found in the weekly charts of smaller companies.

Table 4	Basic LSI Buy Patterns		
Pattern Name	**Pattern Description**	**Pattern Duration**	**Buy Point**
"1-2" Combination	Initial and second spike, upward LSI line	Days to Weeks	Positive Divergence
Stair-Step	Series of primary positive spikes	Weeks to Years	Positive Divergence
Aggressive Stair-Step	High frequency of positive spikes	Weeks to Months	Positive Divergence

Chart Series 43—BBBY

Our three chart example series begins with a look at major retailer Bed Bath & Beyond roughly two weeks after the S&P 500 and Dow Industrials bottomed in March 2009. This daily, one-year "before" chart (43-A) shows a relatively trendless LSI line, which is remarkable considering the impact the economy and depressed level of consumer spending had on retailers. A lone positive spike at 1 buoyed BBBY shares following their actual low in November 2008, but the overall flat trajectory of the LSI line indicates that institutional investors remained on the sidelines.

One month later, in April 2009, institutional investors are visible becoming aggressive buyers of BBBY as confidence grew that the economy had the ability to recover. BBBYs "during" chart (43-B) indicates the formation of a demand imbalance corresponding with the creation of a buy signal. While the stock has appreciated roughly 15 percent since our initial view in March (Chart 43-A), we nonetheless find a far more favorable environment to own BBBY shares anchored by a demand imbalance trend, as confirmed by the small spikes at 2 and 3 and a primary spike at 4. (Note: As a result of the magnitude of the positive spike at 4, which expanded the vertical axis of the chart, spike 1 appears diminished in Chart 43-B when compared with 43-A.)

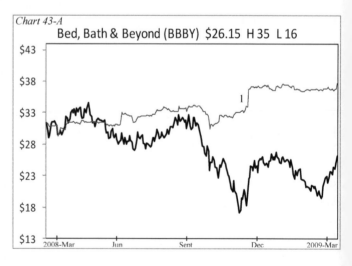

Chart 43-A
Bed, Bath & Beyond (BBBY) $26.15 H 35 L 16

For investors eager to get back into the market through a larger company following the Financial Crisis, the spike at 4 confirms the earlier spikes to produce a 1-2 spike combination pattern.

LSI ANALYSIS: The appearance of a confirmatory spike at 4 presents a buying opportunity in BBBY shares. Investors would buy shares into the first positive divergence pattern (trend line A in Chart 43-C).

Chart 43-C of BBBY, six months "after" the buy signal, shows another positive spike at 5 and five positive divergences (A-E) that provide additional buying opportunities for investors. As a reminder, positive divergences are created by a decline in share price against a flat or positive LSI line and serve as opportunities to buy stocks, according to LSI analysis. For those who recall the extreme level of investor anxiety during the Financial Crisis, investors who could set aside emotions and identify pure demand imbalances would find a fairly typical positive LSI pattern under way in Chart 43-C that corresponded with a great opportunity to buy BBBY shares.

Chart Series 44—HAR

Chart 44-A features the LSI trend from January 2012 to January 2013 of S&P 500

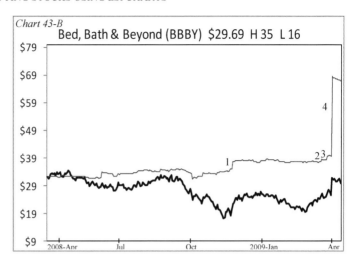

Chart 43-B
Bed, Bath & Beyond (BBBY) $29.69 H 35 L 16

Chart 43-C
Bed, Bath & Beyond (BBBY) $39.79 H 40 L 16

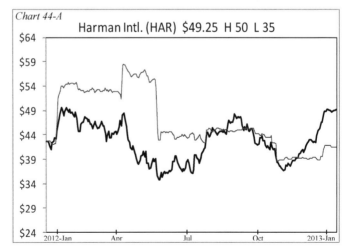

Chart 44-A
Harman Intl. (HAR) $49.25 H 50 L 35

member Harman, maker of the popular Harman/Kardon audio systems. This chart shows a largely trendless LSI line with isolated spikes up and down. Over this period, Harman was recovering from an auto industry still in tatters that accounted for seventy percent of its business. Despite a minor positive spike toward the end of the chart, the trajectory of the LSI line continues to slope downward making this chart unappealing to investors.

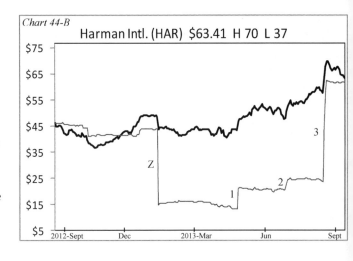

Chart 44-B

Harman Intl. (HAR) $63.41 H 70 L 37

Taking a look at Harman eight months later (Chart 44-B), in September 2013, shows a solid demand trend in place with positive spikes (1 through 3) and an upward trajectory of the LSI line. With auto sales improving, institutional buyers began speculating on Harman shares ahead of an operational turnaround. A buy signal occurs following spike 3 to complete a 1-2 spike combination. Spike 3 is of a magnitude large enough to shift the LSI line trajectory from negative to positive.

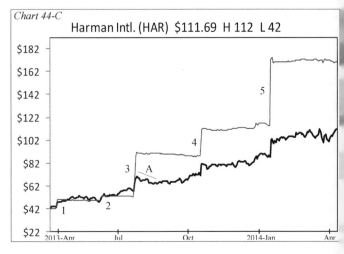

Chart 44-C

Harman Intl. (HAR) $111.69 H 112 L 42

LSI ANALYSIS: Despite the consecutive positive spikes at 1 and 2 in a "1-2" spike combination, the buy signal for Harman occurs following the positive spike at 3 which results in a trajectory shift of the LSI line from negative to positive. Investors would purchase Harman shares into a positive divergence following spike 3 (trend line at A in Chart 44-C).

Returning to Harman in April 2014, Chart 44-C depicts a classic Stair-Step pattern following the initial buy signal at spike 3. Positive spikes at 1 and 2 are somewhat imperceptible now as the scale of the chart has elongated from a high of $75 in Chart 44-B to $182 in this example. The scale has increased because of the magnitude of spikes 3 through 5. We find several small positive divergences after the initial formation at A, and a significant upward rise in share price.

Chart Series 45—CBS

Roughly three months after the market bottomed in March 2009, daily LSI Chart 45-A shows the wreckage caused by an institutionally driven supply imbalance in CBS stock. CBS shares hit a lowly $3 in early 2009, highlighting the steep price declines experienced by heavily leveraged companies during the Financial Crisis. While this chart remains under the influence of a supply imbalance, faint signs of hope appear with the small (micro) spikes at 3 and 4. However, at this early stage, LSI chartists would immediately scan and discard CBS in search of other opportunities.

Two months later, Chart 45-B reveals a growing confidence among institutional investors in CBS. The strong magnitude of the positive spike at 5 changes the trajectory of the LSI line from

Chart 45-A

CBS Corp. (CBS) $6.91 H 17.83 L 2.89

Chart 45-B

CBS Corp. (CBS) $9.28 H 15.17 L 2.89

Chart 45-C

CBS Corp. (CBS) $12.49 H 12.49 L 2.89

negative to positive, indicating the shift from a supply imbalance to a demand imbalance. The large spike at 5 also confirms the small spikes at 3 and 4 to create a buy signal in CBS shares. This chart illustrates that turnaround patterns can begin with subtle signs of positive behavior prior to a confirmatory spike.

LSI ANALYSIS: The positive spike at 5 confirms spikes 3 and 4 to aggregate a 1-2 spike combination. Investors would buy CBS on the first positive divergence following spike 5 (trend line A in Chart 45-C).

Chart 45-C presents a more classical appearing Stair-Step pattern as a result of additional spikes at 6 and 7. A strong demand imbalance is now in place that includes three positive divergence buy points at A, B, and C.

Chart Series 46—SPWR

Chart 46-A shows one of the solar market's highest flyers, SunPower, thudding back to earth by the end of 2012 as an industry-wide supply glut undermined pricing. This weekly, five-year chart shows institutional investors abandoning SunPower in 2008 before a strange, five-year flatline set in, as its shares ultimately dropped from $145 to a low of under $4. By December 2012, investors would have looked past this chart as uninteresting.

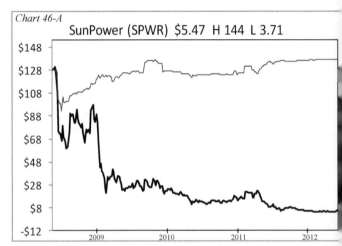

Three months later, Chart 46-B reveals a sudden burst in institutional buying in SunPower on anticipation of a turnaround. Two prominent spikes at 1 and 2 indicate the formation of a demand imbalance and the return to a more favorable investing

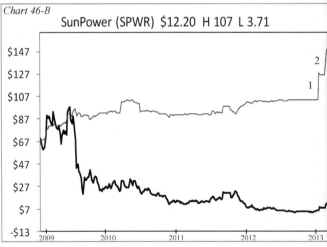

environment in SunPower. These spikes occurring in rapid succession result in an upward trajectory of the LSI line to confirm a buy signal in the stock.

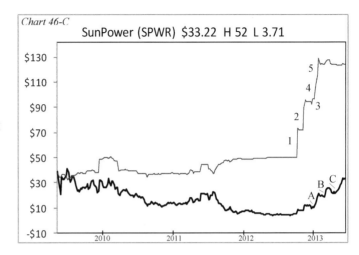

Chart 46-C

SunPower (SPWR) $33.22 H 52 L 3.71

LSI ANALYSIS: Following the confirmatory spike at 2, a 1-2 spike combination is completed and investors would buy SunPower shares into the first positive divergence (trend line A in Chart 46-C).

Chart 46-C in October of 2013 reveals a strong demand imbalance following the arrival of spikes 3 through 5. Positive spikes 4 and 5 occur consecutively, one on top of the other, which is a highly bullish institutional indication that often forms the foundation of a Ladder pattern. Three positive divergences (A through C) of short duration form to create a small window for investors to buy SunPower shares.

Chart Series 47—PSMT

PriceSmart was a stock largely abandoned by investors in 2006 as an operator of Price Clubs in Latin America. The company was spun off in 1997 from warehouse retailing pioneer Price Club, the predecessor of Costco. This weekly, five-year Chart 47-A shows a remarkable two-and-a-half-year period of an absolute flat LSI line (trend line Z), which indicates the absence of institutional

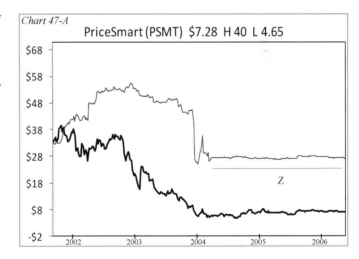

Chart 47-A

PriceSmart (PSMT) $7.28 H 40 L 4.65

activity. LSI chartists would quickly scan and reject PriceSmart shares due to a lack of investor interest.

Just two months later in June of 2006, Chart 47-B reveals an exciting upward move in the LSI line resulting from three quickly forming spikes (1 through 3). These spikes occur over a one-month period, revealing the rapid development of a demand imbalance in the stock. This eye-catching upward move in the LSI line indicates institutional position-taking based on the resumption of same store sales growth at the company's key Price Club locations in Central America and heavy Insider buying in the stock.

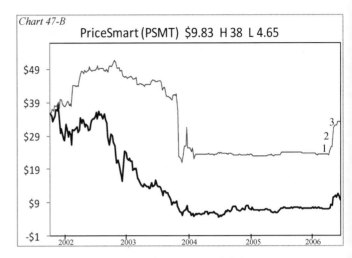

Chart 47-B
PriceSmart (PSMT) $9.83 H 38 L 4.65

LSI ANALYSIS: The LSI chart of PSMT signals a buy following the two positive spikes at 1 and 2 to form a 1-2 spike combination, and was further reinforced by the small spike at 3. These shares would be purchased into the first positive divergence, which occurs during the share price decline at A on Chart 47-C.

Eighteen months later in December of 2007, Chart 47-C shows a dramatic surge in institutional buying of PriceSmart shares following the initial 1-2 spike combination. The LSI line experiences six additional spikes (4 through 9), which includes a minor negative spike at 5 that bears no influence on the upward trajectory of the LSI line. Two additional buy signals occur

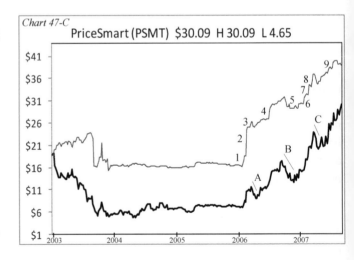

Chart 47-C
PriceSmart (PSMT) $30.09 H 30.09 L 4.65

at B and C following the initial positive divergence formation at A. Chart 47-C vividly displays the power of positive spike activity following a long absence as a major demand imbalance took hold in the stock. PriceSmart eventually topped $125 per share in 2013 following the opening of several new locations that fueled a significant increase in revenue and earnings.

Chart Series 48—RAD

By 2013, the shares of large retail pharmacy Rite Aid had become a case study of a failed turnaround that continued to disappoint investors.

The LSI line in Chart 48-A shows almost four years of directionless activity, with isolated positive and negative spikes culminating in relatively neutral share price behavior. Flat LSI lines indicate an equilibrium of supply and demand, or lack of imbalance. Early in Chart 48-A we find Rite Aid emerging from a low of $0.20 after the Financial Crisis with three spikes (1 through 3), taking the stock briefly above $2 before sellers returned. Investors considering RAD should note two small spikes at 4 and 5 that combine to produce a minor upward slope in LSI line trajectory, but would await confirmatory spikes before entering the stock.

Chart 48-B reveals the emergence of a major demand imbalance following several consecutive spikes (4 through 8). The upward trajectory of the LSI line shows institutions were again willing to bet on a turnaround in Rite Aid shares.

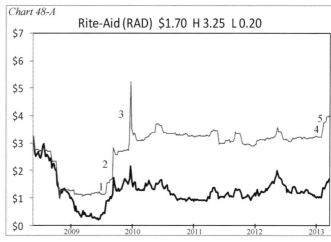

Chart 48-A
Rite-Aid (RAD) $1.70 H 3.25 L 0.20

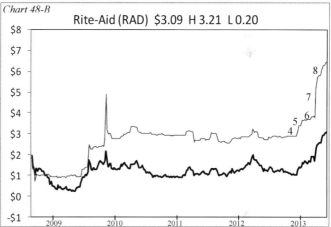

Chart 48-B
Rite-Aid (RAD) $3.09 H 3.21 L 0.20

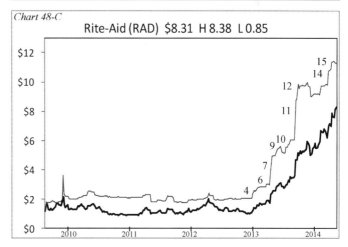

Chart 48-C
Rite-Aid (RAD) $8.31 H 8.38 L 0.85

LSI ANALYSIS: Investors would purchase RAD shares into a positive divergence following the spike at 7 that confirms a 1-2 spike combination.

One year later, Chart 48-C reveals a particularly strong demand imbalance under way through a multitude of spikes. Three positive divergences are visible, two of which are driven by small or minor negative spikes, but which do not negatively influence the upward trajectory of the LSI line. Positive divergences that result from small negative spikes carry a slightly higher degree of risk, but remain buying opportunities if the LSI line's overall trajectory retains its upward heading. The strength of the LSI line ascent in Chart 48-C would appear to finally affirm the long awaited turnaround in Rite Aid.

Chart Series 49—DXYN

While the Financial Crisis in 2008 brought a number of industries to their knees, the home remodel market supplied by high-end carpet makers such as Dixie Group was particularly hard hit. Chart 49-A shows that even as late as 2013, four years after the Financial Crisis, there was still very little interest in Dixie shares. Though a primary spike at 1 is a positive indication and shifts the LSI line trajectory upward, the lack of a confirmatory spike as well as a smaller negative spike (2) would give investors pause. Chart 49-A would be of interest to LSI chartists, although the positive spike at 1 would require further confirmation

By June of 2013, Chart 49-B receives a positive jolt from two primary spikes (3 and 4)

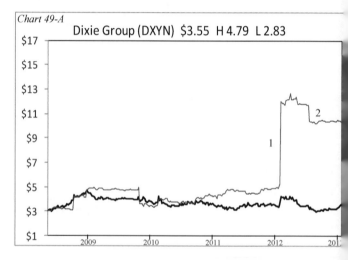

Chart 49-A

Dixie Group (DXYN) $3.55 H 4.79 L 2.83

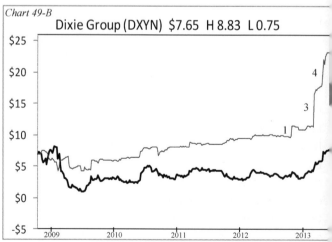

Chart 49-B

Dixie Group (DXYN) $7.65 H 8.83 L 0.75

60

that drive the LSI line into a highly positive ascent. These spikes indicate a strong demand imbalance under way in the stock, corresponding with the first consistent level of institutional buying in more than five years. Chart 49-B also indicates that instead of spike 1 being an isolated event, it was actually the first in a series of spikes (1

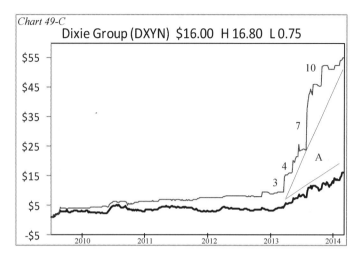

Chart 49-C

Dixie Group (DXYN) $16.00 H 16.80 L 0.75

through 4). While spike 3 can now be considered confirmatory to the initial spike at 1, more conservatively it is spike 4 that confirms the "1-2" spike combination for investors. Note that spike 1 now appears muted as the scale of the chart has increased.

LSI ANALYSIS: Following the confirmatory spike at 4 to define a 1-2 spike combination, Dixie shares would be purchased into the first positive divergence.

Chart 49-C in March 2014 displays a classically positive LSI line pattern common in smaller stocks with an aggressive series of spikes. There are five additional spikes visible, as well as a highly bullish **ascending delta**, whereby the LSI line moves higher at a more rapid rate than the share price (trend lines at A). The multitude of small positive divergences provide a number of opportunities for investors to purchase shares into weakness. Chart 49-C is a solid example of an aggressive Stair-Step pattern, indicating the presence of a major demand imbalance.

Chart Series 50—BLDP

We now move farther down the risk curve to review the LSI chart of fuel cell maker Ballard Power in early 2013. Ballard shares were circulating among just a few sellers, as evidenced by a slow decline of the LSI line in weekly Chart 50-A. Although there appears

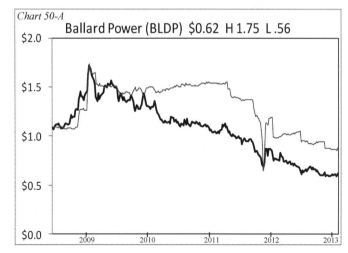

Chart 50-A

Ballard Power (BLDP) $0.62 H 1.75 L .56

61

to be a number of negative spikes in a consecutive downward pattern, note the muted scale along the vertical axis of the chart that more accurately indicates a lack of activity. LSI Chart 50-A would be quickly discarded as uninteresting.

We find an entirely different picture emerging on Chart 50-B only a few months later, as speculation grew that Ballard fuel cells were to be deployed by several clean energy customers. Two sets of consecutive spike formations develop at 1 and 2, and then at 3 and 4, in rapid succession, indicating the development of a strong demand imbalance. Both of these 1-2 spike combinations (spikes 1 and 2

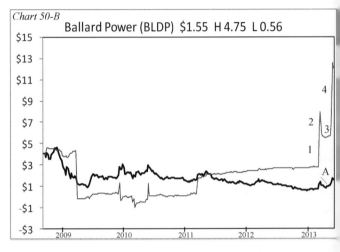

and spikes 3 and 4) are confirmatory patterns that would prompt investors to buy into subsequent share price weakness. Following the spikes at 2 and 4 are bullish formations called **barbs**. Barbs are sharp downward spikes that occur immediately after positive spikes but are of a far lesser magnitude, resembling the barb of a fish hook. Despite their downward heading, barbs indicate heightened volatility and are often the companions of aggressive spike patterns such as Ladders. The appearance of barbs provide confirmation of a highly favorable investing environment.

LSI ANALYSIS: Ballard shares would be purchased into a positive divergence (trend line A) following the initial 1-2 spike combination (spikes 1 and 2).

By March of 2014, Chart 50-C reveals a surge in share price as a result of four additional spikes, culminating with a major spike at 8. Ballard's LSI chart is another example of the aggressive spike patterns associated with smaller stocks that often develop rapidly and lead to explosive increases in share price.

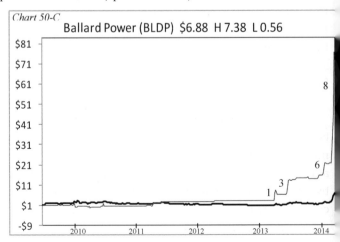

Chart Series 51—IG

Tiny IGI Laboratories (now Teligent) moves us even farther down the market capitalization spectrum from previous examples to highlight the potential for explosive LSI activity, as Charts 51-B and 51-C reveal in this series. As discussed in Chapter 1, the LSI line can rise dramatically when a small stock experiences a major increase in institutional ownership over a relatively short period of time. This aggressive buying results in significant demand imbalances in an underlying stock, as revealed by dramatic spike patterns.

In early 2013, generic pharmaceutical developer IGI Labs held a lowly market cap of only $50 million and was an orphan of the institutional community at only 9 percent of total shares held. By the end of this chart series in March 2014 the LSI line reveals a jump in institutional ownership to more than 20 percent of total shares outstanding. However, despite all of the action ahead, an initial look at IGI in Chart 51-A would be met with a quick wave of the hand from investors.

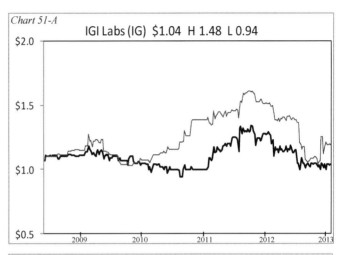

Chart 51-A
IGI Labs (IG) $1.04 H 1.48 L 0.94

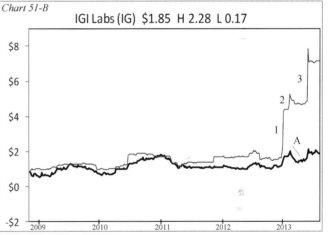

Chart 51-B
IGI Labs (IG) $1.85 H 2.28 L 0.17

Chart 51-B eight months later in October of 2013 captures the excitement just as it begins to build with three spikes (1 through 3) over a two-month period. We also see a major decoupling of the LSI line from the share price — a highly positive development after more than four years of traveling in virtual lockstep — along with an upward trajectory. Positive spikes 1 and 2 combine to create a buy signal, and spike 3 further confirms the formation of a demand imbalance.

LSI ANALYSIS: The 1-2 spike combination (spikes 1 and 2) signals a buying opportunity into the positive divergence that immediately follows (trend line at A). The spike at 3 provides additional confirmation for buyers during ensuing positive divergences.

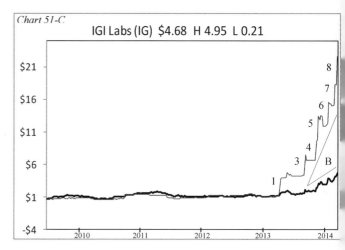

Chart 51-C

IGI Labs (IG) $4.68 H 4.95 L 0.21

The LSI trend in March 2014 that appears on Chart 51-C, just four and a half months later, features an exciting upward march of spikes, and a corresponding surge in share price as IGI began to generate sales of its new topical generics. The pattern of spikes continues upward virtually unabated through spike 8. The lone exception is a small negative spike, which is noteworthy but bears no influence on the LSI line's positive trajectory. There are a couple of additionally bullish features to be noted in Chart 51-C, including a significant ascending delta (B). The other is the relative steepness of the Stair-Step pattern, which is Ladder-like in appearance but lacks the rapid succession of spikes required. Chart 51-C represents a vivid example of the type of LSI activity associated with small stocks that experience sharp increases in institutional ownership.

Chart Series 52—PXLW

One of the more visually striking LSI spike patterns appeared in the LSI Chart 52-C of Pixelworks, a maker of enhanced video streaming software for mobile gadgets. In May of 2013, however, Chart 52-A was largely unappealing following several months of inactivity, which were preceded by a couple of starts and stops along the LSI line. A series of five spikes (Line Z)

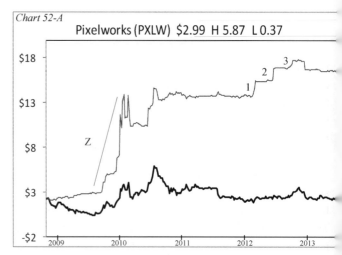

Chart 52-A

Pixelworks (PXLW) $2.99 H 5.87 L 0.37

successfully lifted PXLW shares from a lowly price of $0.37 during the depths of the Financial Crisis before yielding to the period of generally choppy activity that followed.

Spikes 1-3 indicate a tiny Stair-Step forming on the LSI line, although micro and minor spikes tend to be discounted in small companies, and a negative spike subsequently broke the formation. Overall, Chart 52-A would be classified as uninteresting to investors.

This all changes for Pixelworks with Chart 52-B in September of 2013. The chart displays two primary spikes that are confirmatory in a 1-2 pattern (spikes 4 and 5) and produce a significant jump in the trajectory of the LSI line. It is important to note the increase in scale of the chart along the vertical axis, which rises to 32 from 18 in Chart 52-A, highlighting the large magnitude of the spikes at 4 and 5. Accentuating the bullishness of these spikes are barbs, or negative retracements of the LSI line discussed in Ballard (Chart 50-B) that immediately follow both spikes.

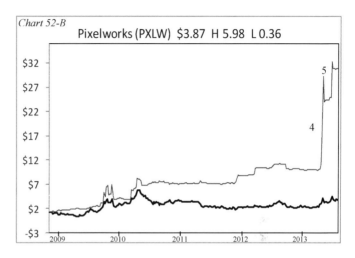

LSI ANALYSIS: The magnitude and confirmatory nature of the 1-2 spike combination at 4 and 5 create a buying opportunity into the first positive divergence following the spike at 5.

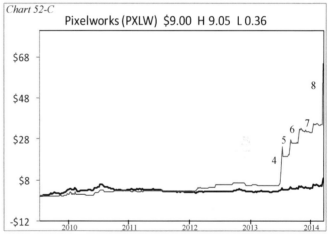

Just six months later, in March of 2014, the LSI chart of PXLW at 52-C shows a spectacular array of spikes (4 through 8), indicating a major demand imbalance driven largely by speculation that Apple would deploy Pixelworks software into its new iPhone. The large magnitude of spike 8 following the multitude of previous spikes is particularly noteworthy, as the chart scale soars to 68 in Chart 52-C. While positive divergences are more difficult to detect in this example due to the magnitude of recent spikes, they are plentiful and follow each new spike.

Using LSI Power Patterns to Buy Stocks

Wings, Ladders and Waves

With a review of 1-2 spike combination buying patterns now under our belt, we are armed with the tools to identify some of the most powerful and exciting of all LSI patterns. These patterns are known for their distinctive formations and bear a close resemblance to the names given of Wings, Ladders, and Waves. As discussed in Chapter 1, these major demand imbalance patterns are the most sought after by LSI chartists for their immediate influence on share price and association with a number of the stock market's biggest gainers. These patterns are also among the easiest to identify, due to their unique appearance and explosive pattern of development. LSI power patterns tend to be most prevalent during emerging bull markets or periods of market recovery, as risk appetite increases and institutions confidently seek out the next big growth stocks. The power patterns in this section are discussed in order of rising demand imbalance and corresponding influence on share price.

Wing Patterns

LSI Wings are patterns that develop with two primary characteristics. First is the appearance of a primary or major (Wing) spike that typically occurs following a period of flat to neutral LSI line activity. The second is the development of an ascending delta. Ascending deltas form as an LSI line rises at a more rapid rate than that of the share price, resulting in a widening chasm between the two lines. Demand imbalances that form under Wing patterns are typically slow to develop, but become increasingly powerful as more and more share supply is siphoned from the market. Wing patterns are named for their resemblance to the outstretched wing of a bird, and become more recognizable as they develop. Although they are more gradual in nature than Ladders and Waves, Wings are powerful indicators of future share price movement.

Table 5	LSI Power Patterns		
Pattern Name	**Pattern Description**	**Duration**	**Buy Point**
Wing	Major (Wing) spike followed by an ascending delta	Weeks to Months	Positive Divergence
Ladder	Rapid, consecutive series of spikes, some barbs	Weeks	Immediate
Wave	Ascending gyration of positive and negative spikes	Weeks	Positive Divergence

Chart 53—APSG

LSI Chart 53 revisits ASPG, originally highlighted in Chapter 1, to illustrate a fully formed Wing pattern that developed in the shares of this intelligence monitoring provider following the events of 9/11. We note the characteristic, initial Wing Spike at 1, followed by ten spikes of varying magnitude to elongate the Wing, culminating in another

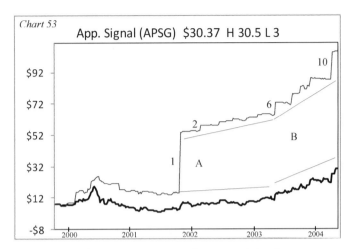

Chart 53

App. Signal (APSG) $30.37 H 30.5 L 3

primary spike at 10. An important signature of Wing patterns is the growth in the magnitude of spikes (6 through 10), highlighting the increasing intensity of the demand imbalance. This increasing magnitude forms an ascending delta that accelerates from A through B. Ascending deltas form where the LSI line rises at a faster rate relative to the share price. Chart 53 represents a classic Wing pattern formation that spans the course of three years.

LSI ANALYSIS: Investors would purchase APSG following the confirmatory spike at 2 into a positive divergence. The long duration of an extended positive divergence should be noted as the LSI line moves higher, providing greater evidence of an emerging Wing pattern. This would prompt investors to add to their positions during subsequent share price declines.

Chart Series 54—CETV

Chart series 54 features a Wing pattern in Central European TV, a fast growing operator of television stations in Romania and the Czech Republic. Prior to the development of a Wing, however, shares of CETV were widely panned by institutional investors in mid-2002, as illustrated by Chart 54-A.

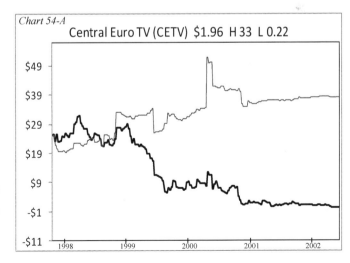

Chart 54-A

Central Euro TV (CETV) $1.96 H 33 L 0.22

CETV shares had crumbled over the preceding four years against a largely indiscernible LSI trend. By 2002, both its shares and LSI line had flattened, characteristic of an unappealing stock.

Almost one year later, Chart 54-B begins to display a growing level of investor interest with a Stair Step-like pattern forming along spikes 1 through 4. At this point it remains unclear if a Wing pattern will develop, but there is ample evidence of a demand imbalance emerging with initial and confirmatory spikes having formed (spikes 1 through 4). It is noteworthy that spike 4 is of much greater

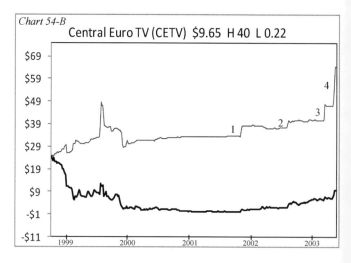

magnitude than spikes 1 through 3. There are no material positive divergences visible as the pattern develops, but it becomes increasingly evident that an ascending delta is forming as the LSI line moves higher at a greater pace relative to the share price. It is during this period we note retrospectively that the positive spike at 4 served as the "Wing" spike, or primary spike forming the creation of a Wing.

LSI ANALYSIS: CETV shares would be considered a buy into a positive divergence formation following positive spikes 3 and 4 in combination, although more aggressive investors may consider 2 and 3 as the buy signal.

By the close of 2004, Chart 54-C features a dramatic Wing having formed with a significant move higher in share price. The Wing spike at 4 has touched off a string of smaller spikes (11 in all), culminating with a primary spike at 15. The Wing in this example formed as a result of a major demand imbalance in CETV shares that grew in intensity over time.

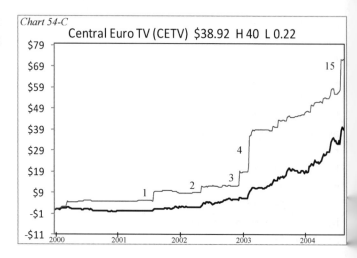

Ladder Patterns

One of the most recognizable and powerful LSI patterns is called a Ladder. Ladders represent highly aggressive buying by institutional investors, over a very short period of time, corresponding with a massive demand imbalance in the stock. A Ladder formation requires three consecutive positive spikes in a "1-2-3" combination. The sheer intensity of buying that creates a Ladder is often reflected in the underlying institutional ownership of a stock, which can grow from a few percentage points of total ownership to as much as 30 to 40 percent over the course of just a few weeks to months as discussed in Chapter 1. Observing such intense buying with LSI charts shows a consecutive pattern of spikes that occur over a condensed time frame. In contrast to the more gradually forming Stair-Step pattern, Ladders arise in a series of dramatic vertical movements on the LSI line resembling a ladder with rungs (spikes) occurring one right after another. Ladders are associated with the emergence of some of the most notable companies in the market, several of which we'll review in the following examples.

Chart 55—WLB

LSI Chart 55 illustrates a fully formed Ladder that developed in the shares of Westmoreland Coal, a Colorado-based coal miner. The Ladder begins abruptly with a spike at 1, following the company's acquisition of another coal producer that doubled the overall size of the company. The spike at 1 is followed by four consecutive spikes (2 through 5) to create a Ladder. There are also bullish barbs

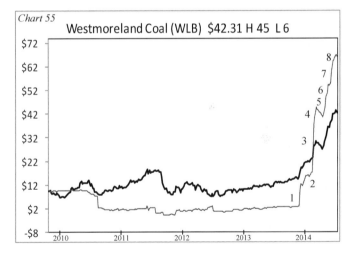

Chart 55
Westmoreland Coal (WLB) $42.31 H 45 L 6

that formed after spikes 2 and 4. These small, sharp declines on the LSI line reflect aggressive buying activity. Ladders form during periods of major demand imbalance, as in the case of WLB, and result from aggressive institutional buying. When viewed closely, this Ladder features eight spikes through a combination of micro, minor, and primary spike formations.

   LSI ANALYSIS: After an initial 1-2 spike combination buy signal, WLB becomes an immediate purchase opportunity following the third consecutive positive spike at 3 that confirmed a Ladder.

Chart Series 56—DECK

One of the most recognizable brands in footwear emerged in 2003 as Deckers Outdoor, maker of the iconic UGG boot, began to gain recognition among retailers. Deckers was a rather sleepy company based in a small California town before the UGG brand became a must-own fashion symbol. An early look at Deckers on weekly Chart 56-A through June 2003 displays four primary spikes spread equally

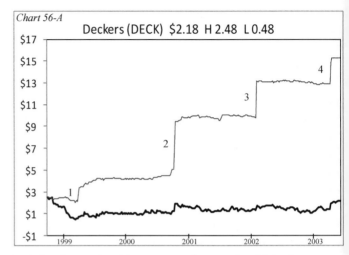

Chart 56-A
Deckers (DECK) $2.18 H 2.48 L 0.48

over a five-year period, yielding a minimal sustained impact on share price. This chart indicates the likelihood of some early adopters taking positions in the stock, but still escaping the mainstream of institutional investors. Chart 56-A would catch the attention of investors, although its spike pattern remained rather spread out over several years.

Chart 56-B serves as the game changer for Deckers in the form of a rapidly developing Ladder pattern. The formation of spikes in this example continues from the previous chart and includes the addition of spikes 5 and 6 ahead of a Ladder pattern created by spikes 6 through 8. Note the distinctive barbs following the spikes at 7 through 9, which reflect

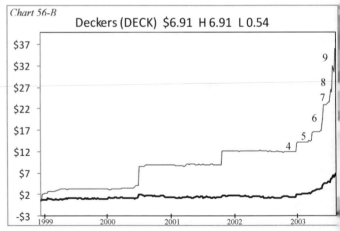

Chart 56-B
Deckers (DECK) $6.91 H 6.91 L 0.54

aggressive buying. While the share price of Deckers appreciates along with the developing Ladder, the pattern reveals a major demand imbalance in the stock, which is a powerful indication of still higher prices to follow. In this example, the spike pattern preceding the formation of a Ladder indicated the presence of a minor demand imbalance that developed into a far more powerful imbalance.

LSI ANALYSIS: Investors would initially buy Deckers on the first 1-2 combination of spikes at 3 and 4, or 4 and 5, as these are in closer proximity to each other. The stock becomes an immediate buy following the 6-7-8 Ladder pattern of three consecutive spikes.

A review of Deckers one year later on Chart 56-C in December 2004 shows the development of numerous additional spikes resulting from the demand imbalance, as well as a strong follow-through in share price. The 6-7-8 Ladder was followed by spikes at 9 through 12 before we see a negative spike at 13, slowing the share price ascent briefly, before resuming with spikes 14 and 15. The Ladder

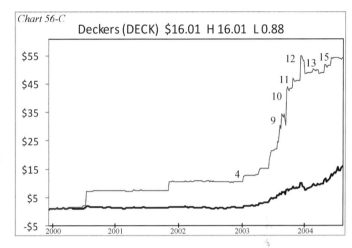

Chart 56-C

Deckers (DECK) $16.01 H 16.01 L 0.88

pattern of Deckers highlighted the emergence of the company on Wall Street, and today UGG remains one of the market's most recognizable brands.

Chart Series 57—LCI

A spectacular Ladder pattern developed in the shares of Lannett, a generic drug maker, in 2013. As is typically the case however, the LSI chart of Lannett prior to the fireworks was an uninteresting case of institutional apathy. Early in 2013, Chart 57-A was dominated by a large negative spike at 1 and subsequent two years of flat LSI line behavior, indicating an equilibrium of

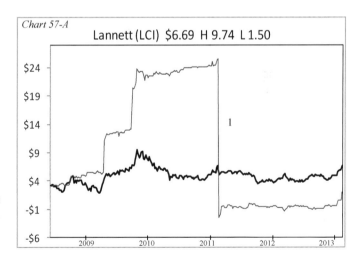

Chart 57-A

Lannett (LCI) $6.69 H 9.74 L 1.50

supply and demand and sign of little institutional interest in the stock. While most investors would move past this chart to look for more interesting patterns, a faint glimmer of what was to come is evidenced by two small (micro) spikes appearing at the end of the chart in quick succession, warranting potentially more than a casual glance.

Just 45 days later, on Chart 57-B, three additional spikes occurred one right after another (spikes 3 through 5), creating a three-spike Ladder pattern. Small barbs are evident following spikes 3 and 5, highlighting the aggressive level of institutional buying in Lannett shares over this period. The major demand imbalances indicated by Ladders, such as in this

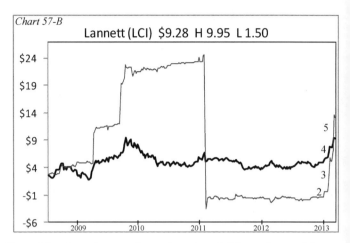

example, signal a higher probability of further share price gains ahead. These favorable probabilities associated with Ladder patterns are what make them so exciting to LSI chartists upon discovery.

LSI ANALYSIS: Shares of Lannett become a buying opportunity immediately following the third consecutive spike at 5 to complete the formation of a Ladder through spikes 3-4-5. Looking ahead, another buy signal occurs in Lannett following a second Ladder pattern created by the combination of spikes at 10 through 15 depicted below in Chart 57-C.

A review of LCI one year later, on Chart 57-C, features one of the most exciting examples of consecutive spikes found on LSI charts. This strong upward surge in demand activity actually formed two Ladders, the first coming with spikes 3-4-5 and then a second Ladder formed by spikes 10 through 15. There is such a rapid occurrence of consecutive spikes in this example that it

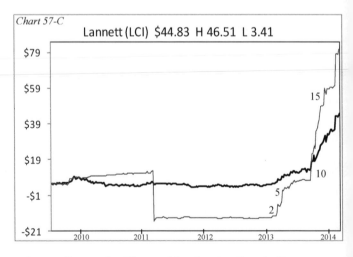

becomes a challenge to identify each one discretely. The multitude of spikes indicates a massive demand imbalance created through a broad grouping of institutional buyers. These patterns found in Lannett represent an ultra-rare combination of two Ladders on a single LSI chart.

Chart Series 58—FARO

Prior to a surge in institutional buying in mid-2003, FARO Technologies, a maker of laser systems for product inspection, was a neglected stock. Chart 58-A features a prominent negative spike at Z and generally neutral overall LSI line activity that would lead LSI chartists to look elsewhere.

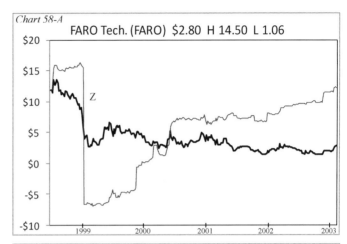

Chart 58-A

FARO Tech. (FARO) $2.80 H 14.50 L 1.06

Chart 58-B, however, reveals an exciting Ladder pattern under way as sales of its laser systems rebounded with the improving economy in 2003. The Ladder is distinctive for a particularly steep ascent of the LSI line that rockets upward on the strength of five spikes occurring virtually in unison. The rapid rise of the LSI line eventually leads to the creation of an ascending delta (trend lines at A), revealed below in Chart 58-C.

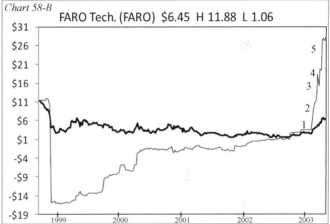

Chart 58-B

FARO Tech. (FARO) $6.45 H 11.88 L 1.06

LSI ANALYSIS: FARO becomes an immediate buy following consecutive spikes at 1-2-3 that combined to form a Ladder.

Chart 58-C reveals a surge upward in the LSI line after formation of the Ladder. The ascending delta seen here is an

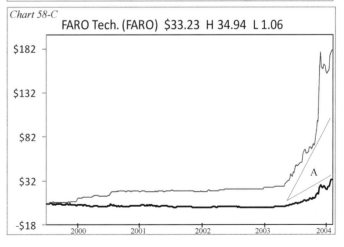

Chart 58-C

FARO Tech. (FARO) $33.23 H 34.94 L 1.06

especially striking example as the LSI line rises at a much more rapid rate than the share price. Ascending deltas serve to "lift" stocks higher as excess supply is eventually taken out of the market. The multiple barbs present along the Ladder highlight an aggressive degree of buying and the strong demand imbalance that formed in FARO shares over this period.

Chart Series 59—USNA

Another strong example of a Ladder that led to the formation of an ascending delta is found in the LSI chart of nutritional product maker USANA. An interesting facet of this Ladder is that it developed during difficult market conditions in mid-2002, in contrast to their more common occurrence during bull markets and periods of market recovery.

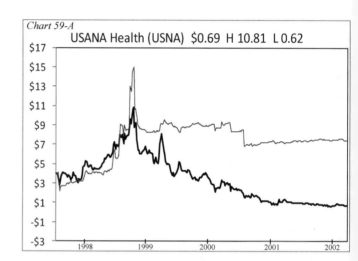

Chart 59-A shows USANA mired in a deep downturn following a peak in late 1998. USANA shares were reaching new lows on the heels of three negative spikes over a four-year period. The LSI line reaches a virtual flatline over the last two years of the chart, rendering it uninteresting to investors.

In mid-2002, however, an exciting series of spikes formed rapidly to create a Ladder. Chart 59-B reveals five spikes (1 through 5) combining to form this Ladder which propelled the LSI line upward. There are two small barbs visible among these spikes, accentuating the bullishness of this pattern. Chart 59-B highlights a major demand imbalance that formed as institutional

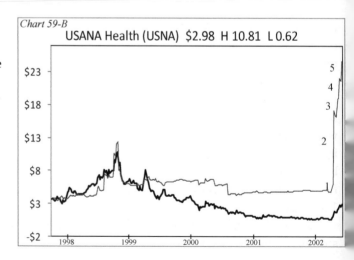

investors aggressively took positions.

LSI ANALYSIS: USANA shares became an immediate buying opportunity following the third consecutive spike at 3 that confirmed the creation of a Ladder pattern.

LSI Chart 59-C features a remarkable Ladder pattern coupled with an ascending delta (A). The ascending delta

Chart 59-C

USANA Health (USNA) $25.07 H 25.07 L 0.62

forms as the Ladder develops and eventually lifts the share price of USANA higher as we see in the latter part of the chart. A string of spikes and a rapidly rising LSI line create a spectacular pattern, which remained in place for more than one year.

Chart Series 60—PCYC

We close our review of Ladders with the dramatic example of drug developer Pharmacyclics (PCYC) to demonstrate the sustained impact these patterns can have on the underlying share price of a stock over a long duration.

A quick scan of the largely negative LSI line pattern in weekly Chart 60-A shows the

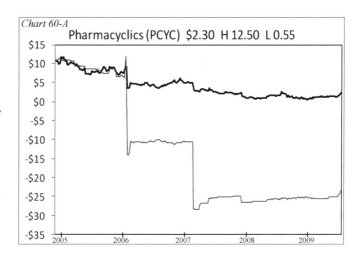

Chart 60-A

Pharmacyclics (PCYC) $2.30 H 12.50 L 0.55

institutional pattern of PCYC before all of the excitement began. Moving ahead several months later to Chart 60-B we find the development of a fully formed Ladder pattern through consecutive positive spikes 1 through 6.

LSI ANALYSIS: Shares of PCYC became an immediate buying opportunity following spike (3) to form a Ladder pattern.

75

Fast forward two and a half years later and we find PCYC as one of the best performing stocks in the market. Chart 60-C in October 2012 shows that following a flat period on the LSI line after formation of the Ladder, a renewed surge in buying took place, launching the stock to $70.

By early 2015 PCYC had soared to a staggering high of more than $200 per share. As this example so vividly reveals, major demand imbalances uncovered by Ladders indicate an increasing scarcity of shares as institutional buyers rush to take positions, providing the fuel to push share prices higher. The LSI chart sequence of PCYC demonstrates why Ladder discoveries can be so thrilling, as well as rewarding.

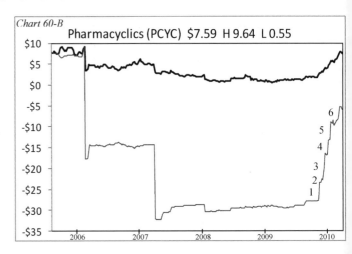

Chart 60-B
Pharmacyclics (PCYC) $7.59 H 9.64 L 0.55

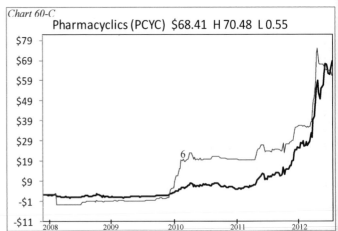

Chart 60-C
Pharmacyclics (PCYC) $68.41 H 70.48 L 0.55

Wave Patterns and Other Bullish Oddities

Among the patterns covered in this chapter we highlight one of the most distinctive formations on LSI charts, a Wave. Wave patterns develop through sharp up-and-down gyrations of the LSI line that often resemble the s-waves and p-waves found on a seismograph during an earthquake. Waves feature an initial primary spike followed by a series of positive and negative spikes occurring rapidly in a tight range and lasting on average a few weeks. These patterns are somewhat of an anomaly, with an equal sequence of negative spikes pairing with positive spikes, while still indicating the presence of a major demand imbalance. As the name suggests, Wave patterns are often associated with violent moves in share price, accompanied by a remarkably high probability of share price appreciation after their formation. These patterns are also rare, unfortunately, and our review contains only a handful of examples.

Chart Series 61—BALT

Chart 61-A serves as the precursor to the formation of a Wave pattern and shows the LSI line of iron ore shipper BALT to be listless and uninteresting to investors.

A Wave pattern begins to form in Chart 61-B with a minor spike at 1 and larger spike at 2, followed by a series of positive and negative spikes of declining magnitude. It is interesting that the share price remains subdued during formation of the Wave and actually decreases following its completion. However, with an aggressive demand imbalance in place, Baltic shares are poised for gains as revealed in Chart 61-C.

LSI ANALYSIS: Investors would buy BALT into share price weakness (positive divergence) following completion of the Wave pattern.

Chart 61-C shows the LSI trend three and a half months after completion of the Wave pattern, revealing a strong jump in share price. The LSI line moves upward after the Wave on additional spike activity. There are two share price pullbacks following the Wave that provide positive

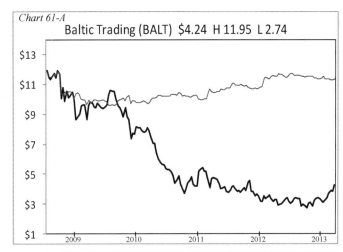

Chart 61-A
Baltic Trading (BALT) $4.24 H 11.95 L 2.74

Chart 61-B
Baltic Trading (BALT) $4.65 H 12.02 L 2.76

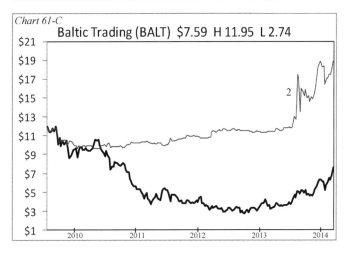

Chart 61-C
Baltic Trading (BALT) $7.59 H 11.95 L 2.74

divergences for buyers. The LSI chart of BALT provides a classic example of Wave pattern formation.

Chart Series 62—BITA

After quickly scanning and rejecting Chart 62-A of Chinese Internet company BITA, we move to Chart 62-B, which shows an exciting spike pattern developing. Although varied and somewhat abbreviated in comparison with the previous example of Baltic, the Wave developing in BITA is clearly visible. This Wave begins with a large spike at 1, followed by a sharp downward barb-like spike at 2. A smaller positive spike then occurs at 3, followed by a very small downward spike at 4 to complete a short duration Wave. Following the Wave, we note a Ladder-like series of spikes (5 through 7), indicating a large demand imbalance present in BITA.

LSI ANALYSIS: Shares of BITA would be purchased during a positive divergence following completion of the Wave (spike 4).

Chart 62-C features a confirmation of the Ladder pattern from the preceding chart, providing additional evidence of the massive size of

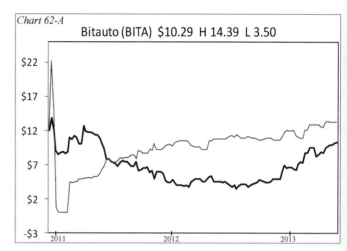

Chart 62-A

Bitauto (BITA) $10.29 H 14.39 L 3.50

Chart 62-B

Bitauto (BITA) $21.73 H 22.37 L 3.50

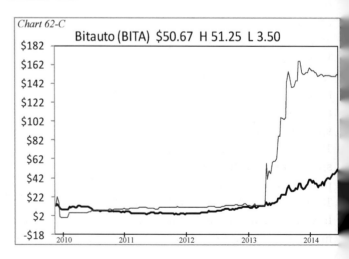

Chart 62-C

Bitauto (BITA) $50.67 H 51.25 L 3.50

the demand imbalance occurring in the stock. This behavior is the result of initial institutional buying that began with the Wave pattern in Chart 62-B. BITA shares begin to climb in earnest following the Ladder and eventually rise to more than $50 on a strong sequence of spikes. The LSI chart of BITA provides a unique example of a Wave that continued to grow in intensity to ultimately produce a Ladder.

Chart Series 63—MNST

An iconic brand to emerge in the early 2000s was Monster Beverage, maker of the popular Monster Energy drink originally featured in Chapter 1. Prior to the launch of Monster, the company was a small, unnoticed drink maker called Hansen Natural. Chart 63-A shows Monster shares beginning to attract attention in 2003 as the LSI line decouples from the share price

Chart 63-A
Monster Bev. (MNST) $0.87 H 0.92 L 0.19

to produce a small Stair-Step pattern. Spikes 1 through 4 form an early 1-2 spike combination and reveal the initial stages of a demand imbalance and buying opportunity in Monster shares.

Following these intriguing early signs, Chart 63-B exhibits a striking Wave pattern (spikes 10 through 18) in Monster. The Wave begins with two primary spikes at 10 and 11, followed by a negative, barb-like spike at 12. A positive spike (13) springs immediately back from 12, met by two more negative spikes and then two more positive spikes. Negative spike 18 concludes the Wave pattern.

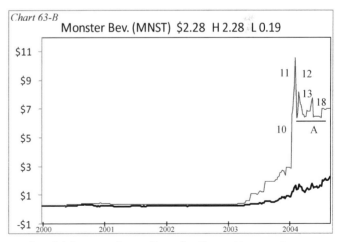

Chart 63-B
Monster Bev. (MNST) $2.28 H 2.28 L 0.19

It is important to note the baseline at A, which served as a floor for the pattern and maintained the upward bias of the LSI line during the Wave. All of these gyrations on the

LSI line signal highly aggressive institutional activity that is usually the precursor of something big to follow.

LSI ANALYSIS: After a buy signal in Chart 63-A with spikes 1 and 2, investors receive a further buy confirmation through a Wave pattern (10 through 18). The downward move in share price following the negative spike at 18 serves as an additional buying opportunity for investors.

Chart 63-C two years later highlights the dramatic increase in share price following the initial buy indication in Monster, as institutional investors became increasingly aggressive buyers. This LSI chart series highlights the magnitude of demand imbalances that can be found with the emergence of a nationally recognized brand such as Monster.

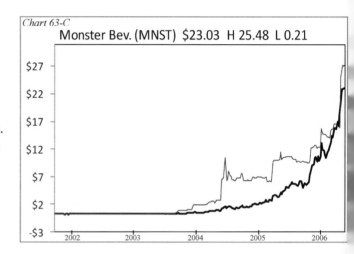

Chart 63-C
Monster Bev. (MNST) $23.03 H 25.48 L 0.21

Chart 64—HCI

A rather odd LSI pattern emerges in Chart 64 of insurer HCI, which was initially featured in Chapter 1. The pattern begins with three spikes (1 through 3), followed by a Wave-like pattern. However, a negative spike at 4 creates some confusion in the formation. The real fireworks begin with major spikes at 5 and 6 and the large associated barbs that propel HCI shares forward. Five additional spikes extend the stock to new highs toward the end of the chart. At the heart of this series of spikes is a major demand imbalance that formed in the stock, resulting in a sixfold increase in share price in less than two years.

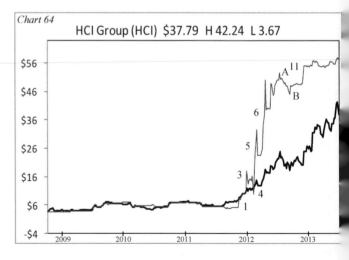

Chart 64
HCI Group (HCI) $37.79 H 42.24 L 3.67

Chart Series 65—ADUS

A final LSI oddity is an interesting Wave featuring a Ladder-like spike and barb pattern found in the chart series of home healthcare provider Addus HomeCare. Thus, is it a Wave or a Ladder? This pattern is distinctive for the multitude of spikes and associated barbs that occur.

Following the lukewarm activity seen in Chart 65-A that would be uninteresting to investors, Chart 65-B reveals the development of several positive spikes, indicating the beginning of a major demand imbalance. Note the sizable barbs that form following the spikes at 1 and 2, which confirm the level of aggressive activity in ADUS shares.

Chart 65-C shows the formation of a Ladder that is made all the more unique by the fact that each of these positive spikes (1 through 6) is followed by a barb. To put Chart 65-C into perspective, more typical LSI charts featuring aggressive buying activity may exhibit barbs on only a quarter to a third of the total spikes in a pattern. ADUS shares continued to climb following the final spike and barb at 6, highlighting the power of these combinations.

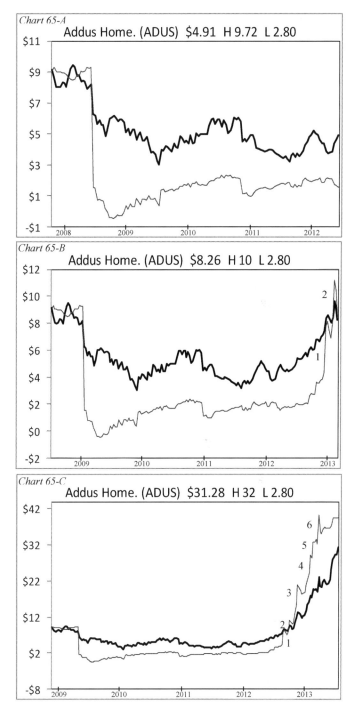

Chart 65-A
Addus Home. (ADUS) $4.91 H 9.72 L 2.80

Chart 65-B
Addus Home. (ADUS) $8.26 H 10 L 2.80

Chart 65-C
Addus Home. (ADUS) $31.28 H 32 L 2.80

Using Turnaround Patterns to Buy Stocks

LSI Bowl, U and V Patterns

Spotting changes in supply and demand, where an imbalance shifts from supply toward demand, can provide investors with a key advantage in attempting to buy stocks at or near share price bottoms. While the old maxim of "never catch a falling knife" is generally a prudent rule for investors to follow when a stock is dropping, it is also difficult for investors to buy a stock after they "missed the bottom." For investors using LSI charts, however, this becomes a fairly straightforward discipline of looking for spike reversals to identify buy points, rather than trying to guess when a stock may have bottomed.

There are three key LSI patterns, called Bowls, Us and Vs, associated with stock turnarounds. These turnaround patterns indicate imbalance shifts from supply to demand that are the basis of stock bottoms under LSI analysis. Bowl, U, and V patterns are generally sought by value investors and bottom-picker's or, as we'll see in Chapter 3, a means of mitigating valuation risk in a portfolio.

Bowls are the most gradual of the three turnaround patterns, typically occurring over several months to years. Bowl patterns feature a reversal of the trajectory of the LSI line from negative to positive, resembling a rounded bowl. Bowls are more commonly associated with large market capitalization stocks, and the gradual nature of the imbalance shift allows stocks to be purchased nearer their price lows. Buyers use positive divergences to enter Bowl pattern stocks.

U patterns are more aggressive turnaround formations, as compared with Bowls. U patterns feature a negative spike that is completed by a positive spike (completion spike) of similar magnitude. This pattern of downward and subsequent upward spikes of similar magnitude is what gives U patterns a symmetrical resemblance to the twenty-first letter of the alphabet. As discussed in Chapter 1, U patterns are similar in appearance and often associated with Bowls. U's take anywhere from a few weeks to rare cases actually taking a couple of years to complete. Investors purchase U pattern stocks into a positive divergence following the completion spike.

The most aggressive turnaround formation is a V pattern. V patterns indicate an immediate reversal from supply imbalance to demand imbalance occurring over the span of several days to a couple of weeks. These patterns are marked by a sharply pointed "V" formed by a negative spike that is immediately followed by a positive spike of similar magnitude, although multiple spikes may also combine to create this pattern. V pattern stocks are immediate purchase opportunities as opposed to the positive divergences required to signal a buy opportunity in Bowls and U's.

Charts 66 through 73 feature Bowl, U and V pattern turnaround stocks that highlight a shift from supply to demand imbalance.

Table 6	LSI Turnaround Patterns		
Pattern Name	**Pattern Description**	**Pattern Duration**	**Buy Point**
Bowl	Rounded pattern of negative to positive spikes	Months to years	Positive Divergence
U	Negative spike followed by positive spike	Weeks to years	Positive Divergence
V	Sharp V reversal: negative spike to positive spike	Days to weeks	Immediate

Bowl Patterns

As discussed, Bowl patterns feature a gradual change in trend from supply imbalance to demand imbalance. This produces a rounded pattern on the LSI line that most commonly occurs in larger cap stocks of the Dow and S&P 500. The gradual nature of the formation allows buyers more time to spot positive divergences in the stock, whereby the share price retreats against a positive to neutral LSI line. As the following examples reveal, Bowl patterns typically occur over several months to years and offer a multitude of opportunistic positive divergences.

Chart Series 66—AMAT

Prior to the formation of a Bowl pattern in the shares of semiconductor equipment giant Applied Materials, Chart 66-A shows a negative path of the LSI line from 2009-2011 despite a share price that rose from roughly $8 to $15. The LSI line continues a downward path, however, representing a minor ongoing supply imbalance in the stock and reflecting a lack of interest in the rally from institutional investors. Chart 66-A of AMAT indicates little overall institutional direction.

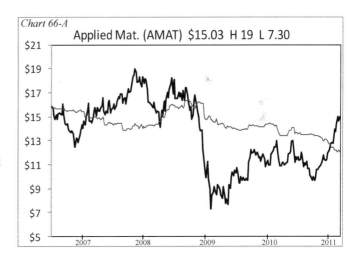

Chart 66-A
Applied Mat. (AMAT) $15.03 H 19 L 7.30

Some two and a half years later, Chart 66-B reveals the first material signs of institutional buying since 2006, as institutions sensed a cyclical uptrend under way. Prior to the Bowl, it is noteworthy to see the paths of share price and LSI line travel in opposite directions, resulting in a large **negative divergence** (trend lines at A). Additional negative divergences follow at B, C, and D, with the share price ascending against a negative, or declining LSI line. Small spikes at 1 and 2, and a slight uptick in the LSI line, are the first indications of a shift in the imbalance trend. The spike at 3 confirms the development of a demand imbalance as institutional buyers return to AMAT shares.

LSI ANALYSIS: Spike 3 confirms spikes 1 and 2, resulting in a Bowl buy signal. AMAT shares would be purchased into the first positive divergence at E, following spike 3, as seen in Chart 66-C.

LSI Chart 66-C shows an extension of the Bowl pattern with a series of spikes (4 through 7). The positive divergence at E is followed by a second buying opportunity

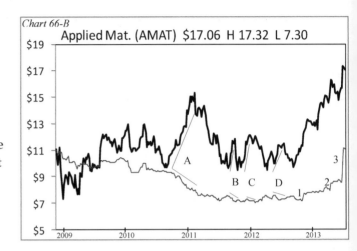

Chart 66-B
Applied Mat. (AMAT) $17.06 H 17.32 L 7.30

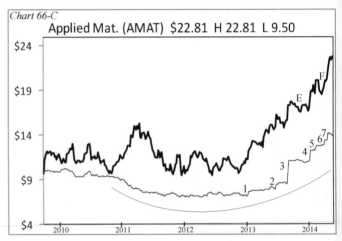

Chart 66-C
Applied Mat. (AMAT) $22.81 H 22.81 L 9.50

at F. Chart 66-C provides a classic example of a completed Bowl pattern, as a supply imbalance gradually shifted to a demand imbalance over the course of three years. As we mentioned in Chapter 1, the LSI line may often trail behind, or lag the share price in larger stocks due to a high level of pre-existing institutional ownership. The upward trajectory of the LSI line is the determining factor in this example of AMAT and in the charts to follow, not its position below the share price.

Chart Series 67—PBI

As discussed at the outset of this section, Bowl and U patterns can appear similar during an imbalance shift. While it can be said that all U patterns typically result in a Bowl pattern, the example of AMAT shows that not all Bowls occur as U patterns. The LSI chart series of PBI features an example of a Bowl forming in conjunction with a U pattern.

By 2012, Pitney Bowes had been largely panned by institutional investors as a company whose postal meters were too closely tied to the faltering U.S. Postal system. Chart 67-A highlights a pervasive supply imbalance lasting over five years, as several prominent negative spikes (1 through 5) develop on the chart. A quick glance of Chart 67-A would send investors elsewhere, at least those not looking for a short sale candidate.

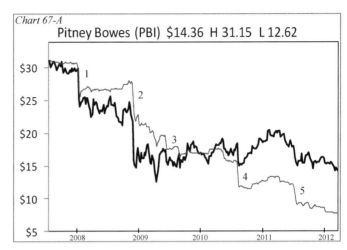

Chart 67-A
Pitney Bowes (PBI) $14.36 H 31.15 L 12.62

One and a half years later, Chart 67-B reveals the beginning of a reversal in the imbalance trend from supply to demand. Prior to the positive activity there were two additional negative spikes (6 and 7), sending the stock below $10 for the first time. While the positive spike at 8 does not reverse the LSI line's negative trajectory, it is notable nonetheless for its magnitude. Following spike 8

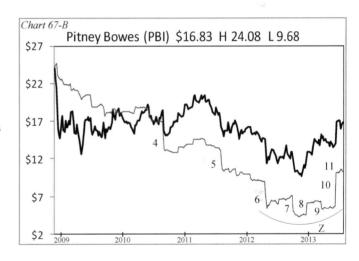

Chart 67-B
Pitney Bowes (PBI) $16.83 H 24.08 L 9.68

is a smaller magnitude negative spike at 9, which, interestingly, does not result in a new low on the LSI line. The positive spike at 10 is the sign investors have been waiting for, as the LSI line's trajectory finally reverses from negative to positive. While the negative spike at 9 may appear to break up the 1-2 spike combination sequence required for a buy signal, we find other signs indicating a buy in PBI. There is evidence of a rounding pattern indicative of a Bowl, as well as a U pattern formed by negative spike 6 and positive spike 10.

LSI ANALYSIS: The shares of Pitney Bowes become a buying opportunity for investors during the first positive divergence formation (A) following completion of a Bowl pattern in Chart 67-C.

85

Chart 67-C shows a well developed Bowl pattern coupled with a U pattern. U patterns can build upon themselves, as we see here with the negative-to-positive spike combination of 6 and 10, followed by additional combinations of spikes at 5 and 12, and 4 and 13. By April 2014, the demand imbalance has increased and the share price has recovered almost all of the lost ground

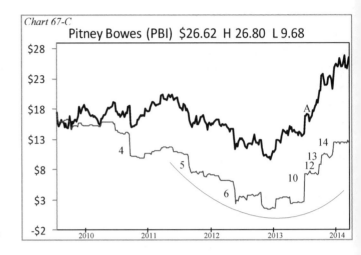

from its previous high of $31 in Chart 67-A. PBI is a classic example of a Bowl and U pattern forming in conjunction to signal the reversal of an imbalance trend.

Chart Series 68—WBMD

Another excellent example of a Bowl and U pattern combination takes place in the LSI chart series of online health information portal WebMD through early 2014. In this example, a series of positive spikes led to a shift in trajectory from a negative LSI line to positive, resulting in the creation of a Bowl pattern that also shared the appearance of a U during formation.

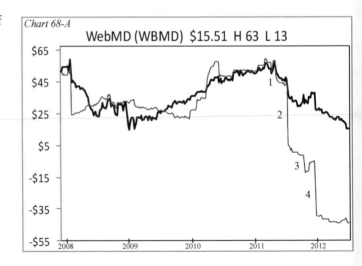

Chart 68-A in August 2012 shows the existence of a large supply imbalance, taking WebMD shares downward from over $60 per share to $15.50 in less than eighteen months. Large negative spikes (1 through 4) highlight the heavy degree of selling in the stock, driven mainly by institutional investors exiting as fears increased over a slowdown in advertising revenue.

A look at Chart 68-B of WebMD nine months later in May 2013 indicates the initial signs of a turnaround in the stock. Beginning with the last leg downward of negative spikes at 4 we find the first positive spike at 5 followed by a second small spike at 6. These spikes combine to produce the initial signs of an end to the negative trajectory of the LSI line. Peeking ahead to Chart 68-C, we find a

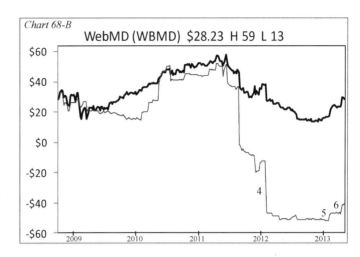

progression of positive spikes (7 through 11) following 5 and 6 that develop into a small spike Stair-Step pattern. A multitude of corresponding positive divergences develop along the LSI line in WebMD shares to produce a total of five buying opportunities (V through Z).

LSI ANALYSIS: The two minor spikes at 7 and 8 on Chart 68-C confirm one another, but their small magnitude relative to the large negative spike at 4 may lend a degree of caution. Nonetheless, the spikes 7 and 8, coming consecutively on the heels of spikes 5 and 6, confirm a buying opportunity for investors into the positive divergence pattern (W) that formed during the price pullback.

In July of 2014, Chart 68-C indicates that institutional buying in WebMD was well under way through an expanding Bowl formation. The addition of positive spikes 9 through 11 provide this chart with a U-like appearance similar to the reversal pattern seen in the shares of Pitney Bowes above. LSI Chart 68-C depicts a completed Bowl pattern at A with several positive

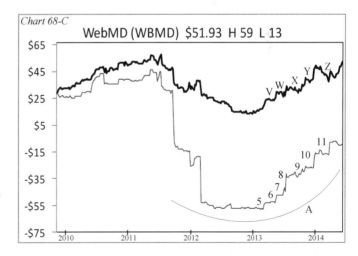

divergence buying opportunities occurring along the course of a significant share price recovery.

U Patterns

In our review of Bowls we discussed a similarity in appearance to U patterns. In the following U pattern examples, it is important to note a key difference in these two patterns, which is one of symmetry. U patterns have a combination of three features on the LSI line: 1) a distinctive negative spike that is followed by, 2) a period of flat trajectory on the LSI line followed by, 3) a positive (completion) spike of similar magnitude to the negative spike. This sequence of features culminates to form a pattern closely resembling the letter "U" in appearance. U patterns indicate an abrupt reversal in the underlying imbalance trend of a stock, from supply to demand imbalance. In contrast, Bowl patterns tend to see a more gradual shift of these imbalances. Thus, U patterns tend to have a greater and more immediate impact on share price than Bowls. Investors purchase U pattern stocks into the first positive divergence following the completion spike.

Chart Series 69—AOL

Shares of AOL, Inc., (formerly America Online) entered the market in a spinoff transaction in 2010, as discussed in Chapter 1. We see in Chart 69-A a history of activity that dates back to February 2011, and thus provides a review of only several months in this weekly chart. This particular chart, with a negative spike at 1, would keep investors awaiting a more positive trend.

Picking up the activity of the LSI line a little more than one year later in April 2012 (Chart 69-B), we note a distinctive U pattern having formed as the company began to transform its business. The U pattern exhibits a negative spike at 2, followed by a flat LSI line at A, and then is

Chart 69-A
AOL, Inc. (AOL) $18.97 H 24.54 L 17.50

Chart 69-B
AOL, Inc. (AOL) $21.21 H 24.54 L 10.16

completed with a positive spike at 4. (Note a small negative spike at 3 that doesn't influence the formation of the U.) It is important to observe the symmetry as discussed above, which makes a U pattern distinctive.

LSI ANALYSIS: The positive spike at 4 that completes the U pattern is confirmatory, and AOL shares would be purchased into the first positive divergence at B.

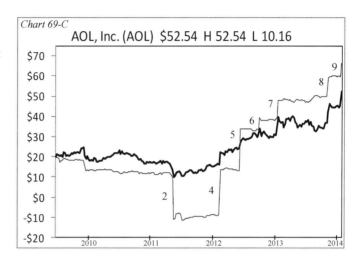

Chart 69-C

AOL, Inc. (AOL) $52.54 H 52.54 L 10.16

Chart 69-C features a progression of spikes following completion of the U pattern. AOL shares rose steadily from $21 on increasing strength of the demand imbalance that followed spike 4. Based on the symmetry and strong magnitude of the spikes completing the pattern at 2 and 4, AOL provides a classic example of U pattern formation.

Chart 70—DXCM

U pattern stocks can also display cascading confirmatory indicators, such as the case of DexCom in Chart 70. DexCom hit the ground running for Type 1 diabetes patients in 2013 with its sleek new continuous glucose monitoring (CGM) pod. Prior to 2013, however, the company experienced growing pains, resulting in a large supply imbalance that knocked its shares from a high of $17 to back under $10.

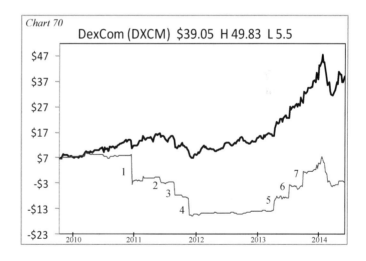

Chart 70

DexCom (DXCM) $39.05 H 49.83 L 5.5

By 2013, Chart 70 shows an initial positive spike at 5. This positive spike was preceded by a long period of flat, neutral activity on the LSI line that followed negative spike 4. The

89

4-5 spike combination completed a U pattern of strong symmetry. What is unusual in the example of DexCom is the rising share price despite a flat LSI line with the stock actually reaching a new high following the spike at 5.

    LSI ANALYSIS: DexCom shares would be purchased into the first positive divergence following the spike at 5 that completes the U pattern.

    Chart 70 also shows a unique sequence of U patterns that developed following the initial 4-5 combination. Additional U patterns in DexCom form in a cascade fashion following the initial formation, with negative-positive spike combinations at 3 and 6, and 2 and 7. Additionally, the positive spikes at 6 and 7 would be considered confirmatory to the positive spike at 5 to form a Stair-Step. This LSI chart is unique for its multiple U patterns, elongated baseline, and upward moving share price during formation.

Chart Series 71 — CSC

Our final U pattern example takes place in the shares of major IT outsourcer CSC, during 2012. Chart 71-A highlights a major supply imbalance associated with institutional selling that was taking place during late 2011 on slumping business awards at its government division. Negative spikes 1 through 5 highlight this supply imbalance, which is uncharacteristically large in magnitude for an S&P 500 stock. During this period, investors would avoid these shares due to the high degree of selling.

    Chart 71-B reveals an initial positive spike occurring at 6 to form a tight, short duration U pattern, consisting of spikes 5 and 6. At first

Chart 71-A

Computer Sci. (CSC) $23.86 H 56 L 24

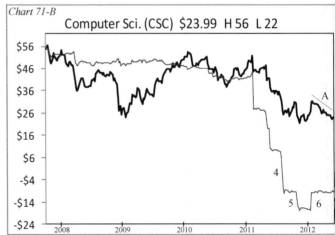

Chart 71-B

Computer Sci. (CSC) $23.99 H 56 L 22

glance the U pattern in this chart is rather unremarkable, considering the small magnitude of the spikes against the significant selling that took place (spikes 1 through 5). In addition, the LSI line's trajectory still appears negative or, at best, to have merely bottomed. Nonetheless, the U pattern in this chart is clearly defined in symmetry and distinctive in appearance following its formation.

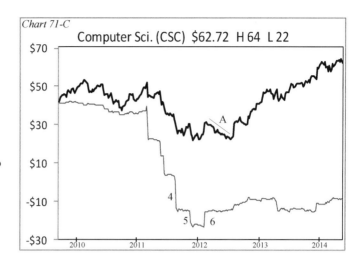

Chart 71-C

Computer Sci. (CSC) $62.72 H 64 L 22

LSI ANALYSIS: CSC becomes a buying opportunity following completion of the U pattern at spike 6 into the first positive divergence that occurs at A.

Looking at the LSI trend of Computer Sciences two years later in Chart 71-C, we find a material recovery in share price, despite a somewhat lackluster LSI line trajectory following the U pattern's completion at spike 6. There are only small spikes visible during this two-year span. However, as we see in this example, U patterns can be powerful predictors of share price movement, particularly when occurring in larger market cap stocks such as CSC.

V Patterns

Following our review above of slower moving Bowl and U patterns, we now turn our attention to the more aggressive and actionable V pattern. To reiterate, Bowl and U patterns are closely related both visually and in their ability to indicate a shift from supply to demand imbalance. In contrast, V patterns form rapidly over the course of a few days to weeks, producing a distinctive reversal pattern resembling the letter of the alphabet. V patterns are formed by a negative spike that is immediately followed by a positive spike of equal or greater magnitude. These patterns represent a rapid and often violent change from supply imbalance to demand imbalance that signals immediate action for investors. V patterns are highly recognizable and strong predictors of future share price movement. But they are unfortunately rare and usually found during times of extreme market volatility.

Chart 72—BEN

The daily, one-year Chart 72 of investment management firm Franklin Resources provides an excellent example of a V pattern forming during the 2008-2009 Financial Crisis. As one would surmise, the rapid decline of the stock market during the height of the recession hit investment management firms hard, as they contended with shrinking investor portfolios caused by market losses and client redemptions. The selling

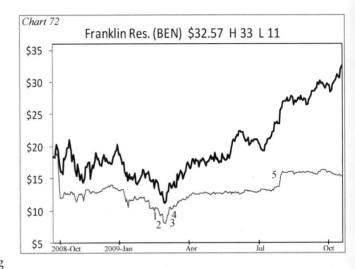

Chart 72

Franklin Res. (BEN) $32.57 H 33 L 11

continued unabated in BEN, as revealed by the negative spikes through March 2009.

The V pattern in this example forms through four rapidly occurring spikes: negative spikes 1 and 2, and positive spikes 3 and 4. Positive spikes 3 and 4 occur consecutively, giving the appearance of a single larger spike. The combination of these four spikes results in an abrupt end to the supply imbalance and immediate shift to a demand imbalance, creating the appearance of a "V."

LSI ANALYSIS: BEN becomes an immediate buying opportunity following completion of the V pattern at spike 4.

Looking at BEN during the latter part of Chart 72 shows a significant increase in share price following the V pattern at spike 4. Except for the multitude of tiny (micro) spikes occurring just after completion of the V pattern, we find only the positive spike at 5 continuing to fuel the share price recovery. The LSI chart of BEN represents a classic example of V pattern formation both in appearance and in its impact on the underlying share price.

Chart Series 73—CP

An interesting V pattern emerged in the weekly LSI Chart 73-B of Canadian Pacific Railway in late 2011. Prior to that, however, Chart 73-A shows a negative LSI trend moving downward in lockstep with the share price throughout early 2009. A significant negative divergence develops over the course of the next two years (trend lines at A) that would have kept new investors at bay.

Chart 73-B reveals a unique V pattern that more closely resembles the appearance of a checkmark. The V in this example is formed by a negative spike at 1 and corresponding positive spike at 2. Though difficult to discern, spike 3 is actually a large spike that occurred immediately after the spike at 2 to produce the checkmark appearance. Nonetheless, the spikes at 1 and 2 serve to form a V pattern that becomes further accentuated by the spike at 3.

LSI ANALYSIS: Canadian Pacific shares became an immediate buy opportunity following the positive spike at 2 that completed the V pattern.

A look at the LSI pattern of Canadian Pacific in Chart 73-C two and a half years later shows a strong follow-through in share price after the formation of the V pattern. There is a minor negative spike at 5 that does not influence the overall upward trajectory of the LSI line. Spikes 6 through 8 confirm an ongoing demand imbalance over this period and combine to produce a minor Stair-Step pattern in the latter part of this chart.

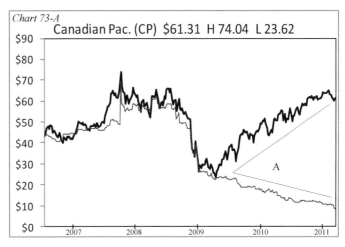

Chart 73-A
Canadian Pac. (CP) $61.31 H 74.04 L 23.62

Chart 73-B
Canadian Pac. (CP) $58.94 H 74.04 L 23.62

Chart 73-C
Canadian Pac. (CP) $182.85 H 184 L 34.12

Conclusion

Using LSI charts to make buying decisions can lead to significant advantages in stock selection as we've seen in Chapter 2, including the ability to capture some the market's biggest winners. Key formations and rules that govern purchase decisions, such as the "1-2" spike combination and upward moving LSI line, arm investors with the tools needed to review a multitude of charts and select the most actionable patterns. From LSI power patterns to more conservative formations, investors can use LSI charts to discover demand imbalances that form at the initial stages of share price gains. With this understanding, we are now ready to move on to Chapter 3 to put LSI charts into practice to trade stocks, take advantage of investment strategies, and build comprehensive stock portfolios. Unique case studies at the end of Chapter 3 provide a bird's eye view of portfolio managers using LSI analysis to run investment strategies. Let's now take a look at LSI charts in action!

Chapter 3

Investment Strategies Using LSI Charts

In this chapter, we apply LSI charts to a broad range of investment and portfolio creation strategies, bringing together all we have learned in the preceding chapters. These investment strategies include trading and options investing, sector and cyclical investing, and sector rotation. Later in the chapter, we review LSI charts during the process of screening and selecting stocks in the creation of portfolio strategies. This includes selection against a defined index or group of stocks to create conservative, growth, and speculative investment portfolios. We then review two strategies using the broad market universe of all stocks with LSI charts as both a screening and stock selection tool to create unique portfolios according to specific patterns.

Chapter 3 demonstrates how investors can optimize the process of both screening and selecting stocks with LSI charts to enhance the overall performance of investment strategies and portfolios. The screening of stocks takes on new purpose as investors can use supply and demand imbalances to further refine a list of potential investment candidates. For the first time, investors can make investment decisions based on knowledge of prevailing institutional sentiment.

In the creation of portfolios, investors typically screen stocks according to a number of fundamental factors, such as revenue and earnings growth, return on equity, and a host of other metrics. Additionally, some investors may use technical factors to screen stocks, looking at trend lines or moving averages appearing on stock charts. Investors can now apply analysis of supply and demand imbalances to portfolio screening. From a list of screened candidates, investors select stocks to buy according to a particular portfolio strategy or risk class. Using LSI charts, investors can now fine tune this selection process by identifying stocks that exhibit the most actionable imbalance patterns. The portfolio examples later in the chapter demonstrate how investors can implement LSI charts to maximize investment returns.

At the conclusion of this chapter, we explore three interesting case studies of investment managers using LSI charts to optimize their proprietary portfolio strategies. These case studies demonstrate how LSI charts can be applied to improve the effectiveness of stock selection. In the first case study, a portfolio strategy focused solely on the S&P 500 incorporates LSI chart patterns to finalize the stock selection process. A second case study features a strategy that screens portfolio purchases through five-year weekly LSI charts before further confirming the timeliness of selections through one-year, daily charts. The final case study reviews a long/short investment strategy created by a hedge fund. This strategy applies daily LSI charts to establish both its long and short positions from a select group of stocks taken from the Dow, S&P 500, and Nasdaq 100 indexes.

We begin our review with the analysis of short-term trading and options strategies using LSI charts before moving on later in the chapter to more complex sector analysis and portfolio creation.

Trading Strategies Using LSI Charts

Our review of investment strategies using LSI charts begins with a look at short-term trading strategies. For active investors who regularly trade stocks, LSI can be useful both as a tool for initially screening or refining a list of trading candidates, as well as in the timing of specific trades. Whether validating a current trading list or creating a new one, traders can use LSI charts to identify stocks that closely follow spike patterns to increase the effectiveness of trades. Stocks that move in close alignment to short-term spike changes can be powerful selections in generating consistent trading profits. In this section, we review how investors can identify stock candidates using daily LSI charts as well as gauge buy and sell decisions to maximize short-term trading profits.

For experienced traders, creating a list of candidates typically involves finding stocks that meet certain criteria, such as average daily trading volume, price volatility, and a host of other metrics unique to each trader. For traders who maintain a list of favored stocks, reviewing past trades against a daily LSI chart is a relatively simple process of back testing to match those stocks whose price performance is most closely correlated to directional spike changes.

The daily LSI chart examples to follow highlight a close correlation between individual spikes and share price movement, to help time long and short trades. We note the effectiveness of using daily versus weekly LSI charts in this process to best identify short-term institutional activity. By following the spike patterns of closely correlated stocks, investors can time buy and sell decisions by simply following changes in spike and LSI line direction.

The daily Chart 74 of Deere and Chart 75 of First Solar are examples of closely correlated stocks that feature differing levels of volatility. These LSI chart examples are shown with share price gridlines, to help identify specific buy and sell prices associated with directional spike changes. In these examples, traders follow the most recent spike direction and bypass such traditional LSI buy rules as the 1-2 spike combination. In our first example of Deere, volatility is low, which may be less appealing to certain traders, but the correlation to spikes is high.

Chart 74–DE

The LSI chart of Deere (74) features spike patterns and share prices over a one-year period from August 2013 to August 2014. According to directional changes in spikes on this chart, four trading opportunities arose over a 12-month period.

Trading opportunity Number One occurs with positive spike 1 at $83.01 on November 20. The long bias of this spike extends over spikes

Chart 74

Deere (DE) $84.09 H 93.90 L 79.94

2 through 4 before closing at $89.19, with the negative spike at 5. This long position (Number One) yielded $6.18, or 7.4 percent, over a 32-trading-day period. Trading opportunity Number Two occurs as a short sale position initiated immediately following negative spike 5 at $89.19. This short position lasts 37 days, along negative spikes 5 through 7, until positive spike 8 marks the closure of this position at $85.89, resulting in a small profit of $3.30, or 3.7 percent. Trading opportunity Number Three is a new long position that begins at spike 8 and is maintained until the negative spike at 12. The conclusion of this trade following the negative spike at 12 results in a gain of $5.20, or 6.1 percent, over 51 days. The final trading opportunity, Number Four in this example, is a short sale position following negative spike 12 at $91.09, extending through negative spike 15 and remaining open at the conclusion of this chart. This price of $83.97 produces an unrealized gain of $7.12, or 7.8 percent, over 74 days.

Table 7	Deere (DE) LSI Trading Summary					
Initiation Date	Position	Spike #	Price	Gain/Loss	% Return	Duration
November 20, 2013	Long	1	$83.01	+$6.18	7.4%	32 days
January 7, 2014	Short	5	$89.19	+$3.30	3.7%	37 days
March 3, 2014	Long	8	$85.89	+$5.20	6.1%	51 days
May 14, 2014	Short	12	$91.09	+$7.12	7.8%	74 days

The theoretical trading gains in this example do not consider commissions and other trading costs. While gains are not fully maximized in this example (selling at the precise top or buying at the bottom), the confirmatory nature of the LSI spikes provides a powerful indicator to generate profitable trades.

Chart 75–FSLR

LSI Chart 75 is a daily one-year chart of First Solar (FSLR), a leading solar player and considered one of the more volatile growth stocks in the market. Similar to the example of Deere in Chart 74, trading opportunities here are based solely on directional changes in spikes and bypass the traditional 1-2 spike combination rule. Traders following this chart would

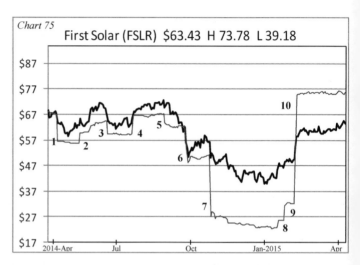

Chart 75

First Solar (FSLR) $63.43 H 73.78 L 39.18

encounter five opportunities over the period from April 2014 through April 2015, according to LSI analysis.

As reflected in Table 8, the first three trades are not highly productive and reflect only minor, short-term buying and selling imbalances in the stock. Trading opportunities Number One through Three occur following the spikes at 2, 3, and 4 and collectively result in a wash in profits. The negative spike at 5, representing trading opportunity Number Four at $69.92, is far more profitable. Following the negative spike at 5 there are additional negative spikes at 6 and 7, taking First Solar shares briefly below $40 in January 2015. The positive spike at 8 that occurred on February 2 closes the short sale position at $45.48. This short sale trade lasted 96 days and resulted in a gain of $24.44, or 34.9 percent. Trading opportunity Number Five is a long position that immediately follows the positive spike at 8 at $45.48 and remains open through the end of the chart. The last quoted price of $63.43 per share results in an unrealized investment gain of $17.95, or 39.5 percent, over a period of 57 days.

By using LSI charts to identify stocks with the highest correlation to changes in spike patterns, traders can generate highly favorable returns over time based on directional changes. Though trading in First Solar began in lackluster fashion, the final outcome of this more volatile stock resulted in two significant trading opportunities over a twelve month period.

Table 8	First Solar (FSLR) LSI Trading Summary					
Initiation Date	**Position**	**Spike #**	**Price**	**Gain/Loss**	**% Return**	**Duration**
June 5, 2014	Long	2	$65.39	($1.00)	(1.5%)	23 days
July 8, 2014	Short	3	$64.39	($1.21)	(1.9%)	21 days
August 6, 2014	Long	4	$65.60	+$4.32	6.6%	27 days
September 15, 2014	Short	5	$69.92	+$24.44	34.9%	95 days
February 2, 2015	Long	8	$45.48	+$17.95	39.5%	57 days

Trading Options Using LSI Charts

The world of stock option investing is far different from that of equities, with important risk considerations such as expiration dates, time premiums, and deltas for investors to consider, none of which applies when trading stocks. In addition, there are a host of strategies relevant only to options, such as spreads, straddles, and fences that make investment positions far more complex than when trading equities. However, the overall goal of identifying the best stock candidates in which to trade options remains. Incorporating LSI charts with the objective of identifying stocks with specific imbalance formations lead options investors to select stocks with the highest correlation to spike patterns.

Introducing LSI charts to option strategies involves the central theme of identifying stocks closely correlated to spike patterns, just as we do when trading stocks. While we'll leave a comprehensive review of options investing to a future volume, there are several notable methods that take advantage of LSI charts when trading options. The most fundamental of these are investors using put and call options in the same fashion stocks were purchased and sold short from our two previous examples of Deere and First Solar. Options investors identify the specific put or call in relation to a particular spike direction, and then select from an options chain based on associated expiration dates. For options investors in Deere, we can see from the preceding table that the average duration of the long and short trading positions is under three months. In First Solar, the two most profitable trades occurred at two and three months duration. Options investors must therefore note the historical trading characteristics involving LSI charts for each stock used in the underlying options strategy.

Investors can also take advantage of divergence patterns on LSI charts to increase the success rate of options strategies. Positive and negative divergence patterns greatly increase the probability of the subject stock moving in a direction that corresponds favorably to the option. Finding LSI charts where stocks are rising or declining in a direction opposite to their respective LSI line pattern can yield strong candidates for options strategies. Buying put options of stocks rising against a negative LSI line (negative divergence) and call options of stocks declining in relation to a rising LSI line (positive divergence) are strategies that take advantage of these patterns. Other LSI chart patterns can be applied to options strategies by using power patterns like Ladders and Waves to speculate on near-term call options, or by using straddles (owning both put and call options simultaneously) to take advantage of high volatility. These are just a few of the examples of options strategies that can be employed in conjunction with directional changes in LSI spike patterns.

Taking the LSI charts of Deere and First Solar from our previous example and applying a put/call options strategy, we arrive at the theoretical trading results found in Table's 9 and 10. In each of these examples, contract expirations of three months in duration are used to maximize the outcome potential according to historical trading characteristics of LSI charts. While it is always important to consider that the value of options contracts can fall to zero, using options in these two examples provides investors with a significantly higher percentage return as compared to trading in the underlying shares.

Table 9		Deere (DE) Option Trading Summary						
Initiation Date	Option	Contract Expiration	Strike Price	Contract Buy Price	Contract Sell Price	% Return	Value of $1,000 Trade
Nov. 20, 2013	Call	Feb. 2014	$82.50	$4.10	$7.65	86.5%	$1,865
Jan. 7, 2014	Put	Apr. 2014	$90	$4.05	$5.70	40.7%	$1,407
Mar. 3, 2014	Call	Jun. 2014	$85	$4.20	$7.25	72.6%	$1,726
May 14, 2014	Put	Aug. 2014	$90	$3.45	$6.05	75.3%	$1,753

Table 10		First Solar (FSLR) Option Trading Summary						
Initiation Date	Option	Contract Expiration	Strike Price	Contract Buy Price	Contract Sell Price	% Return	Value of $1,000 Trade
Jun. 5, 2014	Call	Sept. 2014	$65	$6.75	$5.10	(24.4%)	$755
Jul. 8, 2014	Put	Oct. 2014	$65	$6.20	$4.90	(20.9%)	$790
Aug. 6, 2014	Call	Nov. 2014	$65	$6.80	$7.95	16.9%	$1,169
Sept. 15, 2014	Put	Dec. 2014	$70	$6.35	$24.65	288.2%	$3,881
Feb. 2, 2015	Call	May 2015	$45	$5.65	$18.70	230.9%	$3,309

Whether trading stocks or using options, daily LSI charts can be integrated to execute short-term strategies to improve performance, as well as to decide when to initiate and close positions.

Sector Investing Using LSI Charts: Trucking

Applying LSI charts to specific market sectors can reveal the institutional favorites within an industry group. When a particular sector gains favor, the largest companies typically see the first signs of institutional buying, followed by gradual or, in some cases, aggressive "trickle down" buying into smaller companies. We highlight this trickle down effect in the trucking sector, using a line running through the charts to coincide with an initial large spike (1) on the LSI chart of trucking leader Swift Transportation.

In late 2014, transportation became a major beneficiary of the collapse in oil prices. Truckers experienced a significant windfall as fuel prices plunged, sparking a rally in the sector. Larger, high quality companies led the advance, followed by smaller, more risky competitors. The biggest companies in the trucking sector, such as Swift and JB Hunt, were snapped up by institutional investors looking to invest in the leading opportunities benefiting from lower oil prices.

We look at four companies in the trucking sector using LSI charts in order of descending market cap. A line downward marks the beginning of institutional buying in trucking based on a large initial positive spike (1) in Swift

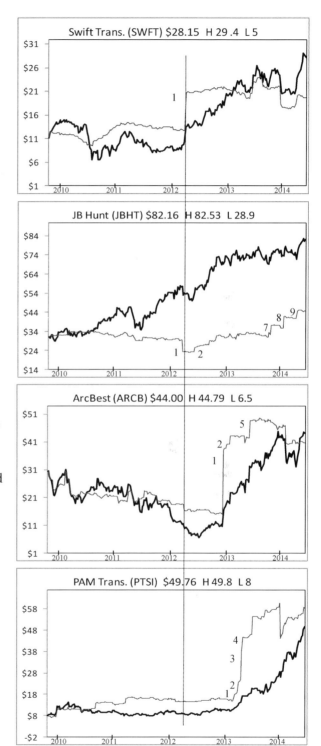

Transportation in late January 2012. Extending a line downward from this spike over the same time period to other sector members reveals the staggered institutional activity that began in larger stocks and then progressively trickled down to smaller companies. Investors tend to move down in risk class as confidence in a particular sector grows and larger companies increase in valuation. Sector investors take their cue from the initial activity among large cap stocks and look for signs of institutional buying in smaller companies. Reviewing individual LSI charts in this example, we find a trickle down to smaller cap stocks that ultimately produced significant demand imbalances including Ladder patterns and other aggressive spike activity.

Among the LSI charts reviewed in this example, we see a strong initial spike in Swift, which marked the earliest institutional trace point in the trucking sector upswing. J.B. Hunt actually shows a small negative spike (1) to contrast with the positive spike (1) in Swift before experiencing a series of small spikes that led to a gradual Stair-Step (7 through 9) pattern. ArcBest and PAM Transportation follow several months after the initial spike in Swift with the first signs of positive spike behavior. ArcBest experienced a large initial spike (1) followed by smaller spikes (2 through 5). PAM is the last company to see institutional buying in this sequence, approximately two to three months after ArcBest. PAM became a buy following a highly bullish Ladder (1 through 4) pattern.

By identifying sector leaders and tracking smaller components using LSI charts, investors can enter positions based on their respective risk classes and take advantage of both early stage and trickle-down demand imbalance trends.

Cyclical Investing Using LSI Charts: Computer Chips

Cyclical industries are well known to investors from chemicals to consumer companies. These sectors run the gamut from autos to semiconductors. Major shifts in institutional sentiment influence cyclical stocks over the span of a few to several years, as they come into and fall out of favor with investors. Tracking imbalance shifts through LSI charts can provide a significant advantage in cyclical investing. Looking at notable members of the highly cyclical computer chip industry over the five-year period from 2009 to 2014 reveals a rebirth in 2013, following a disastrous chip inventory glut in 2011. The resurgence in 2013 ushered in a new cyclical upswing for the industry.

Looking at the chip companies in this example in descending order of market capitalization, we start with semiconductor behemoth Intel. Because it is the biggest component of the chip sector and its stock is one of the most heavily owned by institutions, Intel's LSI pattern tends to be more subtle than that of smaller, less institutionally held stocks. Beginning with the minor positive spike on the LSI line of Intel (1) in late April 2013, a line is drawn downward through the other weekly LSI charts to mark the start of a new institutional buying phase in the sector. However, it wasn't until several months later that smaller chip stocks experienced a follow-through from Intel's initial spike. When a rotation into the chip sector finally begins, with positive spikes occurring in smaller companies, it marks the beginning of a major cyclical uptrend and large follow-through in share prices. The LSI lines of each of these stocks experience multiple positive spikes during this uptrend signaling higher share prices to follow.

Several months after the initial positive spike in Intel, we find aggressive Stair-Step patterns in each of the smaller companies. Smartphone specialty chip makers Skyworks and Tessera each exhibit initial 1-2 spike combinations that build into patterns that appear to be the beginning stages of Stair-Steps, whereas Triquint experienced a small negative spike at 2 prior to a major spike at 3 and significant move upward in share price.

The 2013 chip market rebound provides a robust case study of trickle down institutional activity and increasingly aggressive buying in smaller stocks that occurs later in the cycle. By identifying the largest stocks in a cyclical sector and looking for demand imbalances, investors can exploit cyclical uptrends with LSI charts and benefit from both early stage and trickle down institutional buying trends.

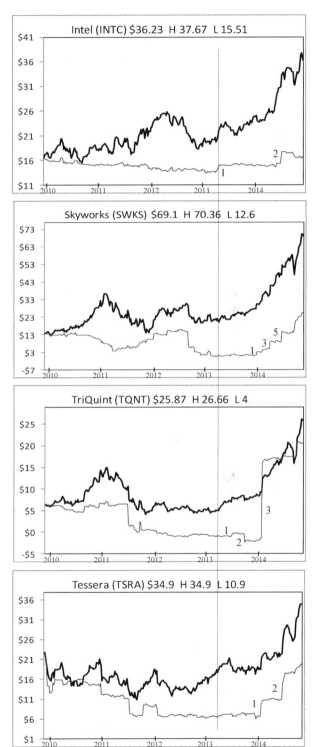

Identifying Sector Rotation Using LSI Charts: Oil Versus Airlines

In our review of sectors and cyclical investing, we have touched on rotation trends that typically accompany an industry upswing. In this example, we'll address institutional sector rotation specifically by looking at the 2014 oil collapse and its beneficial impact upon the airline industry. The LSI charts presented in this sequence reveal the imbalances created by institutional investors rotating into airlines and out of oil stocks.

In this example, we have grouped together airline and oil stocks to show supply and demand imbalances based on the rotating inflows and outflows of institutional investors. While the airline stocks were already experiencing a favorable demand bias as the economy improved, evidenced by positive spike activity (A) in American Airlines and United, correspondingly negative spikes followed later in the oil sector.

Strong institutional buying in airlines began in mid-2013 among larger competitors such as American and United as well as smaller JetBlue and regional operator Hawaiian Airlines (spikes 1 through 3).

While the debacle in the price of crude can be traced to OPECs November 2014 decision to maintain output, institutional selling in oil and gas stocks had actually begun in early 2014.

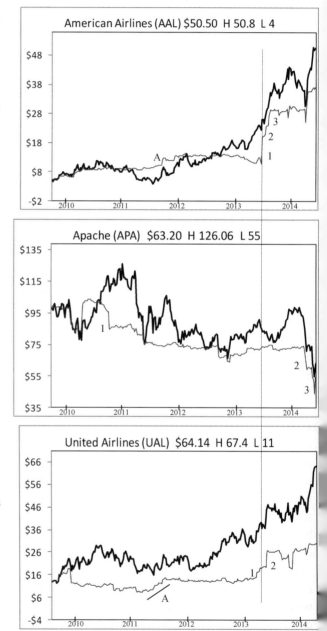

Among energy stocks, large oil & gas operator Apache began to experience significant selling in early 2014 although its shares were already suffering from institutional selling as late as 2011 (negative spike 1). Seadrill's LSI chart shows a moderate degree of selling in mid 2013, based on small spikes 1 and 2, but the major negative spike activity in this stock, as well as C&J Energy, occurred several months later.

Prior to the line running through these charts, institutional investors appeared to be mostly negative on energy, evidenced by negative LSI lines in Apache and SeaDrill, despite rising share prices in 2013. However, the surge in airline share prices contrasts sharply with the negative spike activity among energy stocks that began in the early part of 2014. By the end date of these charts in mid-2014, airline stocks are significantly outperforming energy stocks based on the institutional rotation trends seen months earlier.

These charts demonstrate how investors can apply LSI charts in correlated sectors to spot diverging imbalances and select the most promising stocks. While these sector rotation trends appear to be less traceable to a given point, correlation between divergent sectors increases over time. With LSI charts we can see the initial interest in airlines in relation to lackluster interest in oil, which eventually led to a large divergence among both sectors.

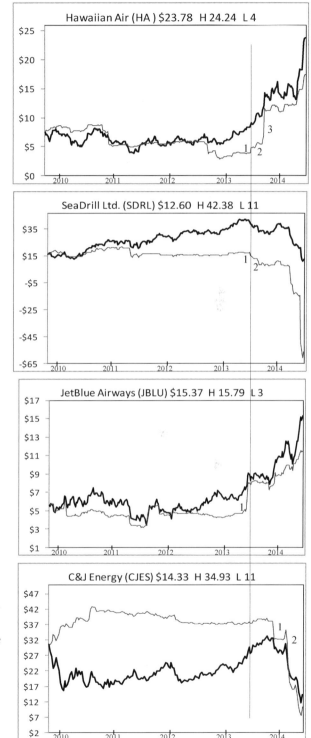

105

Portfolio Creation Strategies Using LSI Charts

LSI charts provide a powerful tool to screen and select stocks in the creation of investment portfolios. In this section, we examine the role of LSI charts as both a tool to refine a previously screened list of investment candidates, and then as a primary stock selection mechanism according to specific patterns. The first three portfolio strategies covered in this section (pages 106 through 111) involve the use of LSI charts as a selection tool from an existing index or predetermined list of stock candidates. The final two strategies (pages 112 through 115) use LSI charts as both the primary screening and selection tool against the broad universe of all stocks. These portfolios are arranged according to investor risk class beginning with conservative, large market capitalization stocks and progressing downward to a portfolio of smaller, speculative stocks.

LSI Conservative Portfolio

To create a portfolio of conservative, blue chip stocks, investors typically screen selections from the lowest risk class groups, such as the Dow Jones Industrials or S&P 100 index. From these indices, investors may screen portfolio candidates according to their own unique criteria, such as fundamental earnings growth, valuation, return on equity, etc. From a list of these candidates, investors can apply LSI charts to further refine stocks based on institutionally driven demand imbalances. As we recall from Chapter 2, conservative stocks typically exhibit far more subtle spike patterns than found in growth oriented stocks. This is because major demand imbalances are less likely to occur in stocks that are already heavily owned by institutions. Therefore, among conservative, large market capitalization stocks, investors would use daily charts to identify demand imbalances.

A sample of eight daily LSI charts is featured on page 107 from a list of conservative, blue chip stocks. In this example, it is assumed these stocks have been pre-screened according to individual preferences, such as the fundamental measures mentioned above. From these LSI charts, stocks presenting demand imbalances appear in bold. While it is noted that some of these bolded stock selections are at varying levels of maturity in their imbalance patterns, all are considered favorable opportunities for conservative investors.

A review of LSI charts of conservative stocks finds demand imbalance patterns in Stocks 1, 4, 5, and 8 (charts highlighted in bold). Stocks 1, 4, and 8 are positive charts that exhibit a more classical Stair-Step pattern. Stock 5 shows initial signs of a turnaround pattern, with three positive spikes after a long period of negative LSI line behavior. Among Stocks 2, 3, 6, and 7 we find neutral to negative trends, with negative Stair-Step patterns found in Stocks 3 and 7. Investors building a conservative stock portfolio would consider Stocks 1, 4, 5, and 8 as portfolio selections and would theoretically add these stocks as initial positions.

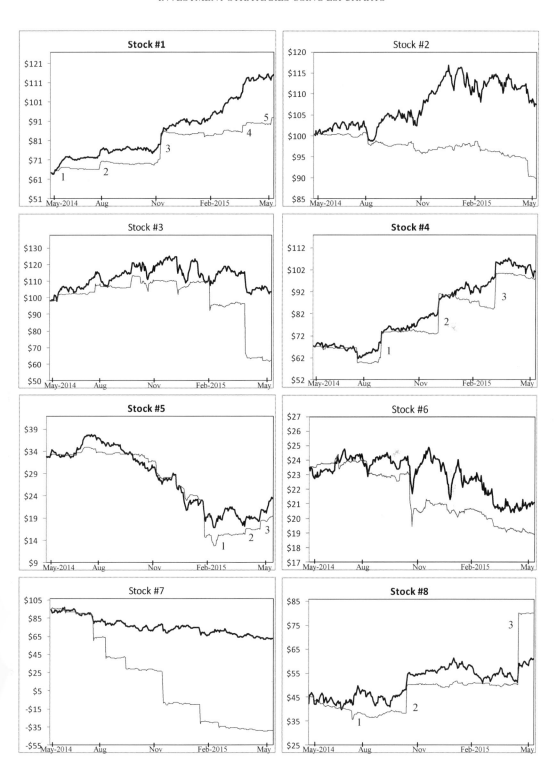

LSI Growth Portfolio

Investors looking to build a portfolio containing growth oriented stocks would screen from an index or group of stocks meeting specific growth criteria. Depending on risk class, more conservative growth investors might choose stocks from an index such as the S&P 500, whereas aggressive growth investors with a higher risk tolerance may choose from a broader market index such as the Russell 3000. In this growth portfolio example, investors would again apply their own set of criteria, as in the Conservative Portfolio above, such as fundamental analysis or valuation metrics, as the initial screen against these indices to generate portfolio selection candidates. LSI charts are then used to finalize the selection process and build a portfolio of stocks that are aligned with demand imbalances. Investors would use daily LSI charts to identify imbalances among the more institutionally held S&P 500 stocks, whereas aggressive growth investors would use weekly LSI charts to choose from members of the Russell 3000 index, which typically contain lower overall institutional ownership.

A sampling of eight daily and weekly LSI charts are displayed on page 109 from a theoretical list of growth oriented stocks of the S&P 500 and Russell 3000 indexes. This group of stocks represents a pre-screened list of candidates that met certain fundamental criteria, according to unique investor preferences. Growth portfolio selections from this candidate list, based on LSI chart analysis, appear in bold, indicating stocks that are presenting demand imbalances. There are varying levels of maturity in these LSI chart patterns, although all would be considered portfolio selections based on strong underlying demand imbalances.

Of the growth stock candidates, Stocks 1, 4, 6, and 7 present positive demand imbalance patterns, representing portfolio selections. Stocks 4 and 6 would likely be indicative of larger market capitalization growth stocks based on the fact that they exhibit classic Stair-Step patterns. Stocks 1 and 7 are more dynamic in appearance, with multiple and more volatile spike patterns. Stocks 2, 3, 5, and 8 all feature negative to neutral LSI line trajectories that would be considered untimely to investors building a growth stock portfolio. Table 11 below outlines growth portfolio additions from these charts according to investor risk class.

Table 11	LSI Conservative/Aggressive Growth Portfolio		
Stock #	# of Spikes	LSI Pattern	Portfolio-Risk Class
1	7	Multi-Spike/Stair-Step	Aggressive growth
4	4	Classic Stair-Step	Conservative growth
6	3	Classic Stair-Step	Conservative growth
7	8	Multi-Spike Positive	Aggressive growth

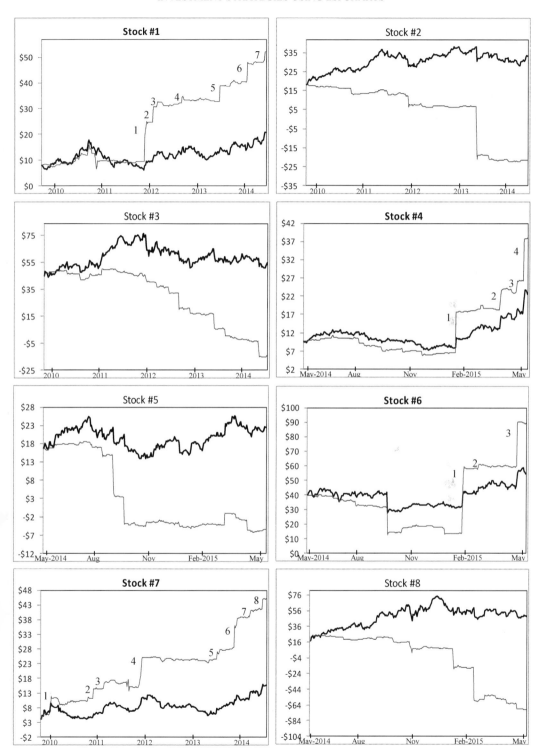

LSI Speculative Portfolio

Building a portfolio of speculative stocks can be accomplished by identifying stocks within broad, small market capitalization indices, such as the Russell 2000 or S&P SmallCap 600. Individual preferences that determine initial candidate screening within these indices can vary widely, as the fundamentals of small stocks tend to be inconsistent or subject to substantial risk. Biotechnology stocks, for example, are typically valued on potential future cash flows, while reporting large current losses prior to a potential drug approval. Initial candidate screening ahead of LSI chart analysis may therefore be difficult or necessitate casting a wide net of fundamental metrics. Following an initial screening process, a list of candidates can then be reviewed according to LSI charts, to determine timeliness based on demand imbalance patterns.

LSI patterns among small, low priced stocks tend to show vivid and sometimes explosive movement on the LSI line, as covered in Chapter 2. These stocks typically possess a very small number of institutionally held shares, meaning that new buying activity can have a dramatic effect on the LSI line. Speculative investors often seek out rapidly ascending Stair-Steps, Waves, and Ladder patterns in this category. A portfolio of stocks containing these LSI patterns would carry elevated volatility, but could also yield some of the highest returns in the market.

A sample of eight weekly LSI charts is featured on page 111. This list of speculative stocks is taken from the Russell 2000 and other small cap indices and pre-screened according to the criteria outlined above. Selections from this list, according to LSI chart analysis, appear in bold, indicating the presence of major demand imbalances.

Among this sample of eight LSI charts, Stocks 1, 3, 5, 7, and 8 all exhibit the highly positive LSI patterns associated with small market capitalization stocks. The most aggressive of these charts is Stock 3, which features a Ladder pattern, and Stock 7, which shows Ladder-like characteristics based on positive spikes 2 through 4. Stock 5 features a multi-spike positive pattern, and stocks 1 and 8 exhibit positive 1-2 spike combinations. Stocks 2, 4, and 6 all display negative to neutral LSI line trajectories and would be avoided. Table 12 provides a theoretical portfolio list based on these charts.

Table 12		LSI Speculative Portfolio	
Stock #	**# of Spikes**	**LSI Pattern**	**Portfolio-Risk Class**
1	2	1-2 Positive Spike Pattern	Speculative
3	9	Ladder	Speculative
5	4	Multi-Spike Positive	Speculative
7	4	Multi-Spike Positive/Ladder	Speculative
8	2	1-2 Positive Spike Pattern	Speculative

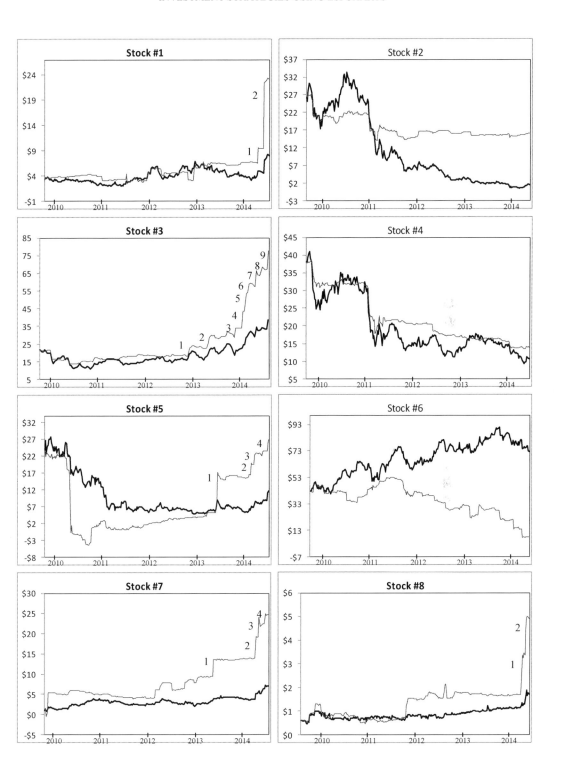

Portfolio Building Strategies Based on Specific LSI Patterns

Growth Portfolio Using Stair Steps

Investors can also establish portfolios that are based exclusively on LSI chart patterns. LSI charts can be used initially to screen stocks according to positive patterns and then to time selections based on specific LSI buy formations outlined in Chapter 2, such as positive divergences. For growth stock portfolios, investors primarily focus on Stair-Step patterns that vary in level of aggressiveness. Conservative growth investors seek stocks exhibiting a more classic Stair-Step pattern, whereas high growth investors look for more aggressive Stair-Steps. Other LSI chart patterns can also be incorporated into a growth portfolio, such as stocks exhibiting a multitude of spikes or a combination of Bowls, U's and V's. Investors may choose any one or a number of these pattern combinations based on risk tolerance. Classic Stair-Steps, aggressive Stair-Steps and multiple spike patterns are predominantly found in stocks that are trading into new share price highs, which tend to imply a higher relative valuation. Bowl, U, and V patterns can be used to offset valuation risk as these patterns typically form in turnaround prospects trading at or near share price lows, implying lower valuations.

The LSI charts featured on page 113 are prospective patterns for investors seeking to create a growth stock portfolio. Stocks 1 and 2 are classical Stair-Step patterns suitable for conservative growth portfolios. Stocks 3 and 4 are higher volatility Stair-Step patterns best suited for aggressive growth portfolios. The multiple spike patterns of Stocks 5 (Wing pattern) and 6 could fit either risk class according to their market capitalization. Stocks 7 and 8 exhibit Bowl and U patterns that can be incorporated into both growth and aggressive growth portfolios, as a valuation counterweight to offset risk. Table 13 outlines these selections according to investor risk class.

Table 13		LSI Conservative Growth Portfolio	
Stock #	Buy-Spike #	LSI Pattern	Portfolio-Risk Class
1	4	Classic Stair-Step	Conservative growth
2	4	Classic Stair-Step	Conservative growth
3	2	Aggressive Stair-Step	Aggressive growth
4	2	Aggressive Stair-Step	Aggressive growth
5	2	Micro Spike	Conservative growth
6	2	Micro Spike	Aggressive growth
7	2	Bowl	Conservative growth-Valuation offset
8	2	U	Aggressive growth-Valuation offset

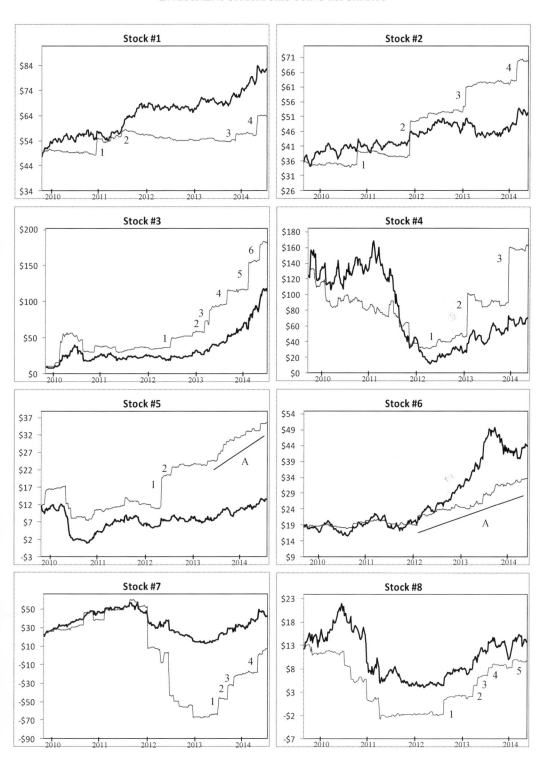

Speculative Portfolio Using LSI Ladders

The use of power patterns to create speculative portfolios, such as in Ladder investing, requires an equal blend of pattern identification and market timing. Power patterns typically arise in the first couple of recovery years following a bear market bottom, for reasons that should be clear to many bargain hunting investors. Blue chip stocks historically lead market recoveries, as investors shun riskier investments in favor of safety. As markets improve so, too, do the prospects of smaller companies that trade at highly discounted valuations. As investors bid up blue chip stocks to higher valuations, bargain hunting usually begins, which can lead to a flood of investment dollars pouring into smaller stocks. Power patterns are rare in maturing bull markets, so it is often under recovery conditions that investors encounter a favorable environment to look for aggressive LSI patterns that include Wings, Ladders, and Waves.

Risk tolerant investors seeking to maximize returns look for specific patterns that result in the highest probability of share price returns. As discussed in Chapter 2, power patterns carry such probabilities and these patterns include Wings, Ladders, and Waves. Speculative investors screen the entire universe of stocks in search of these explosive patterns, to build portfolios generating the highest return potential. Among these patterns, Ladders are the most coveted by speculative investors. Unfortunately, in addition to Waves, they are also among the rarest patterns, due to the tremendous magnitude of the demand imbalance required to produce them. Investors reviewing the entire spectrum of U.S. equities may find fewer than ten Ladders in a given year, depending on the maturity level of a bull market. A portfolio based exclusively of Ladder patterns holds the highest probability of collective returns among LSI chart patterns. However, such a portfolio would also carry the highest degree of volatility. A portfolio based exclusively on Ladders would require a high level of risk management and significant investor experience to maintain a proper balance among positions.

The Ladder patterns profiled on page 115 represent potential selection candidates of a speculative portfolio consisting only of power patterns. Among the Ladders featured in this example set, Stocks 1 through 5 are considered more classical in appearance due to a combination of consecutive spikes, barbs, and steep vertical trajectory of the LSI line. Stock 6 is unique in that it exhibits a 1-2-3 spike pattern before forming a Ladder, which lends a slightly higher degree of conservatism to the pattern. Stock 7 is not actually a Ladder but shows major spike activity that is often the precursor to a Ladder pattern. Stock 8 exhibits Wave-like characteristics that would make this chart interesting to speculative investors. Among these Ladders and near-Ladders, speculative investors can assemble a group of power patterns to create a portfolio consisting of the largest demand imbalances to maximize overall return potential.

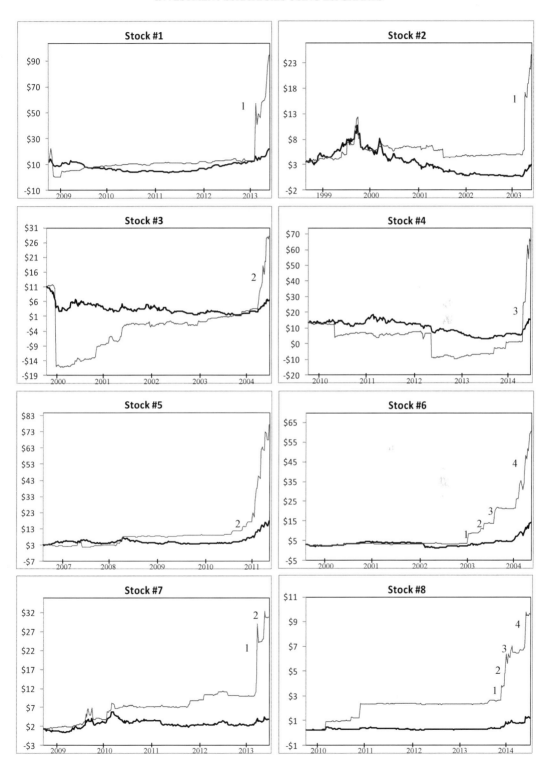

LSI Case Studies—Investment Management Strategies

In this section, we review three case studies of investment managers using LSI charts to create and manage portfolio strategies. These case studies outline the process of analysis and implementation that goes into the creation of a portfolio strategy from the perspective of an investment manager using LSI charts. The case studies reviewed in this section range from a straightforward portfolio of S&P 500 stocks to a complex long/short hedge strategy using selected stocks from several indices.

Case Study #1 — Long Strategy Using Daily LSI Charts

To begin our case study review, we look at an investment strategy focused solely on stocks within the S&P 500 index and analyzed using daily LSI charts. Many investment managers benchmark their performance against specific indices such as the S&P 500 and Russell 3000, seeking to outperform these indexes with a select portfolio of underlying stocks. One of the most popular indexes used by managers to benchmark performance is the S&P 500. Managers who track this index must be mindful not only of stock selection, but also of sector weighting, due to the outsize number of stocks in major industries like technology, healthcare, financials, and energy. These four sectors alone represent almost 60 percent of the entire S&P 500 index. Thus, if a manager is overweight energy but the technology sector is leading market returns, it's a good bet this portfolio is underperforming its benchmark.

With this concept of sector weightings as the backdrop to our first case study, we now review a strategy using S&P 500 stocks and analyzed with daily LSI charts. The investment manager running this portfolio refines the 500 companies of the index based on three separate screens to produce a list of potential candidates. These screens include companies that are 1) the largest market capitalizations, 2) market share leaders in their respective industry groups, and 3) companies that are in the upper 20th percentile of earnings performance within the index. The market capitalization screen reduces volatility by weighting the portfolio toward the largest stocks. The market share leader screen ensures that each industry group is considered. And the earnings performance screen provides a growth orientation to the portfolio. To be included in the list of candidates, each stock must only meet one of these screens. Following the screening process, the investment manager has reduced the overall candidate list to approximately 200 companies from within the S&P 500 index.

The investment manager then exclusively uses daily LSI charts for the portfolio selection process, which can include up to 70 members from the candidate list. By focusing portfolio selection on demand imbalanced stocks through LSI charts, the investment manager increases the performance rate of stocks within the portfolio while improving

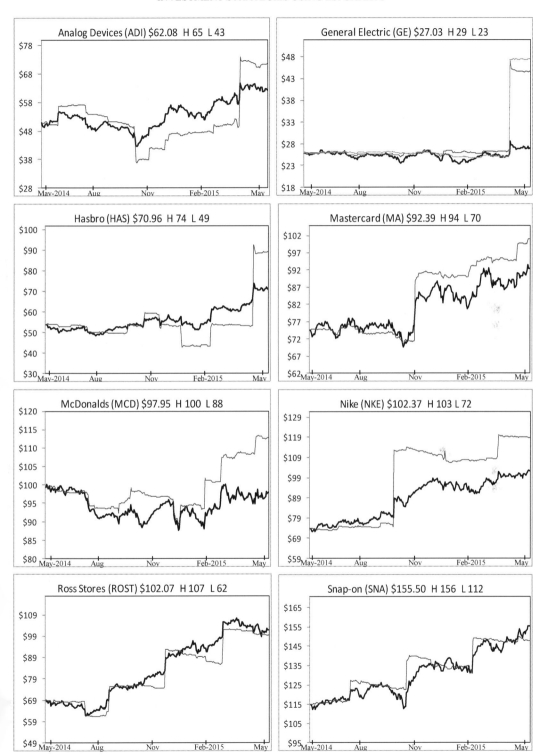

sector weighting within favored industry groups. In addition, the cash component of the portfolio is determined by the number of demand imbalanced stocks selected from the candidate list. In bear markets, for example, the number of stocks with demand imbalances is diminished, leading to a portfolio of fewer than 70 stocks with the balance held in cash. The investment manager in this case study favors Stair-Step patterns among LSI charts, and variations of 1-2 spike combinations that may often feature one initial spike of primary magnitude or greater. A group of prospective charts is featured on page 117. Average turnover of stocks in the portfolio based on this process is 30 percent annually.

Case study #1 serves as a model example of a low complexity growth portfolio. The appealing aspects of this strategy are the defined universe within the S&P 500, intuitive stock screens, and the calibration of market exposure based on the number of demand imbalanced candidates.

Case Study #2 — Long Strategy Using Weekly and Daily LSI Charts in Combination

Our second case study reviews an investment strategy focused on stocks within the Russell 3000, which is a broad market index. The investment manager overseeing this portfolio analyzes stocks from within the Russell 3000 based on a number of technical and fundamental factors to create a candidate list. Selections to the portfolio, comprising approximately 150 stocks, are pulled from the candidate list using a unique combination of weekly and daily LSI charts.

Benchmarking a portfolio against broad market indices that represent thousands of stocks requires a disciplined investment strategy. Creating a candidate list employs many resources, including expensive data feeds and research analysts. Each stock must be screened against the specific investment discipline, presenting challenges in staying current due to changes in corporate events and quarterly earnings reports. Major investment firms such as Fidelity employ large teams of analysts and traders to keep up with the constant changes in stocks and the market. The investment manager in this case study employs three research analysts who analyze candidates according to specific industry groups based on the firm's core investment strategy.

The investment strategy in this study is based on technical as well as fundamental analysis. The technical analysis screen looks for stocks in the upper percentiles of relative strength and stocks holding above their 50-day moving average. Relative strength is a price momentum indicator, and stocks in the upper percentile are currently outperforming the market as a whole. Moving averages of stocks can be found on several Internet websites, including Stockcharts.com. Fundamental factors include specific operational growth metrics such as revenue, earnings, gross margin and operating margin expansion,

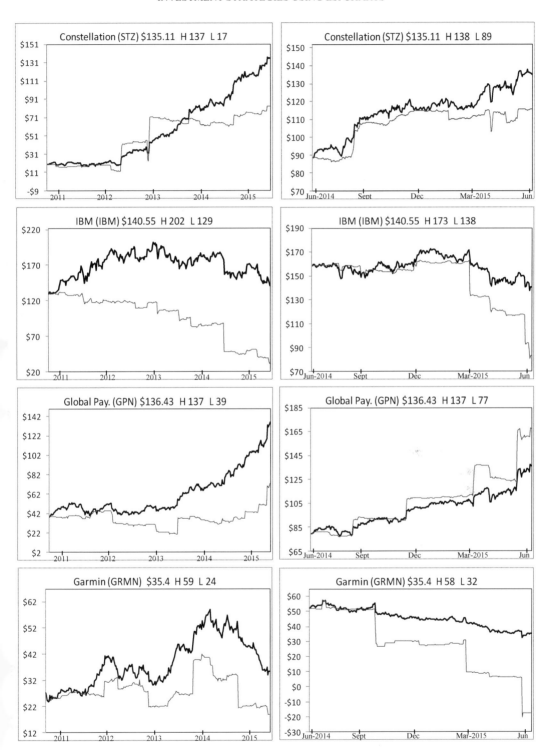

and corporate expansion indicators such as adding new employees, facilities and products. Based on these technical and fundamental screens, hundreds of stocks may reside within the list of investment candidates considered for inclusion into this 150 stock portfolio.

The process of portfolio selection from the candidate list in this strategy incorporates a highly novel and interesting study in the use of LSI charts. In this case, the investment manager runs the candidate list through weekly LSI charts to find stocks oriented toward longer-term demand imbalances. Due to the broad nature of the Russell 3000 index, which includes large capitalization stocks such as Apple, General Electric, and Exxon, as well as small stocks under $250 million in market capitalization, a range of LSI patterns can be found within this index. The investment manager has a stated preference for weekly Stair-Step patterns due to their correlation to the technical momentum screens used in the portfolio, but also dedicates 7 percent of the fund, or about 10 stocks, to power patterns such as Ladders and Waves to generate portfolio outperformance, or alpha. From this screened list of stocks containing demand imbalances on weekly LSI charts, the investment manager then runs this list through daily LSI charts to find selections that are considered timely and immediately actionable to the portfolio.

The LSI charts featured on page 119 are a theoretical list of stocks that have been pre-screened against the technical and fundamental factors outlined above. We have included a weekly, five-year LSI chart (chart on the left-hand side) side-by-side with a daily chart for the same stock covering the most recent 12 months of activity. Among these charts, the investment manager would theoretically select the Stair-Step patterns of Constellation and Global Payments for portfolio inclusion, based on positive weekly charts that are confirmed by positive daily patterns. IBM and Garmin would be rejected due to unfavorable LSI charts exhibiting negative Stair-Step patterns that are untimely both on a long-term and near-term basis.

Case Study #3 — Long/Short Strategy Using Daily LSI Charts

One of the most interesting and effective investment strategies rounding out our review of case studies involves the use of daily LSI charts to buy and sell short stocks from a select group of companies within the Dow Jones Industrials, S&P 500 and Nasdaq 100 indexes. This hedged investment strategy effectively timed the 2008, 2011, and 2015 market downturns and generated positive returns over these volatile periods.

The primary investment thesis of the manager overseeing the hedge portfolio strategy in Case Study #3 is that all market declines are preceded by a breakdown in market breadth, or performance of individual stocks. In other words, stocks begin to show signs of weakening prior to a breakdown in the overall market, such as the S&P 500 index. Identifying these particular signs of an impending market sell-off allows an investor to be prepared in advance of a sustained move downward. Prior to using LSI to implement

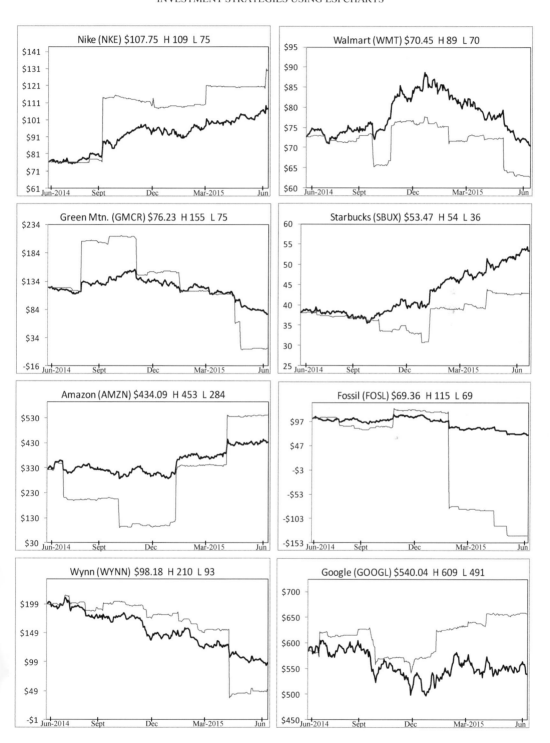

this strategy, the investment manager used technically based stock charting to assess weakening stocks and establish the long/short bias of the portfolio (the number of long positions versus the number of short sale positions). According to the investment manager, the primary drawback of using stock charts was the fact that it was difficult to gauge consolidation versus an actual breakdown in share price. This led to a relatively higher number of false signals and periods of portfolio underperformance versus the market prior to implementing LSI charts.

The investment strategy of the hedge fund in this case study is 100 percent focused on technical factors. The core assumption of this strategy from a fundamental perspective is that focusing on the largest companies within the Dow, S&P 500 and Nasdaq 100 mitigates the necessity of exhaustive fundamental research. The premise is that these companies are among the most heavily researched in the market and fundamental dynamics are already "built in" to their respective share prices. To put it another way, it is too challenging to beat the market on a purely fundamental basis with these stocks due to the high level of existing research. It is therefore more valuable to focus on the technical aspects of these companies. Although a somewhat controversial perspective, it makes sense from the standpoint of a smaller investment fund with potentially more limited resources. The candidate list of this hedge strategy comprises approximately 120 companies from the three major indices, and is based exclusively on their respective correlation to daily LSI chart patterns.

The unique investment strategy of this hedge fund provides a glimpse into the power of using supply and demand imbalances to not only forecast stock prices, but also to gauge market direction. As discussed previously, by simply using stock charts the investment manager had difficulty during certain periods in the market determining whether a stock was consolidating or experiencing a true breakdown in share price. According to the investment manager, LSI charts provide the ability to visually gauge supply imbalances in stocks to improve overall judgment of a consolidation versus breakdown. Thus, instead of focusing on the same price movement that all of the other managers were looking at, this investment manager could shift more quickly to short sell stocks based on the magnitude of underlying supply imbalances to optimize performance. This shift led to a significant improvement in performance of short sale candidates and allowed the fund to better calibrate its weighting of long and short positions.

The candidate list of the hedge fund in Case Study #3 is proprietary, so we have composed a theoretical group of LSI charts that likely mirrored some of the long and short positions of the portfolio heading into the overall market downturn in July 2015. Among the chart examples found on page 121, we find demand imbalances in Nike, Starbucks, Amazon, and Google during this period that would likely comprise the long component of the hedge fund, whereas supply imbalances in Walmart, Green Mountain, Fossil, and Wynn may have constituted short sale positions. Case Study #3 is a prime example of the use of LSI charts in more complex portfolio management.

Conclusion

LSI charts can play an integral role in the screening and selection process of stocks that are purchased as part of investment strategies or to build comprehensive portfolios. Selecting stocks that have a close correlation to spike patterns can improve performance across a range of strategies. These include short-term strategies such as trading and options investing. In sector investing, LSI charts can be used to identify demand imbalances in large stocks that often "trickle down" to smaller stocks. Comprehensive stock portfolios can be created by selecting stocks that exhibit demand imbalances from a candidate list. As the case studies in Chapter 3 demonstrate, LSI charts can be applied directly into the sophisticated portfolios of investment managers to optimize the selection process against a prescreened list of candidates.

Conclusion

Unlocking the dynamics of supply and demand in the world of investing provides an entirely new approach. Investors for the first time can harness the powers of supply and demand to make buy and sell decisions. This book offers an initial glimpse into the capabilities of investing using LSI charts. The realm of interpretation within LSI charts is immense and the patterns outlined in this volume provide only initial building blocks for investors to discover their own unique patterns and features that provide the fuel to propel share prices.

Many subtleties are still to be explored among LSI chart patterns. Patterns such as V's and Wings were only recently "discovered" as being correlated to future share price performance. And different markets produce their own subtleties and interpretations as well. Not only are certain LSI patterns more prevalent at particular maturity levels of bull and bear markets, such as Ladders occurring more frequently following bear market bottoms, but the effects of high frequency and algorithmic trading are being felt in the marketplace. LSI chart patterns evolve with these changes. I recall a weekly Stair-Step pattern for Detroit Edison in 1988 that remained in absolutely perfect formation for the five consecutive years of the chart. I wouldn't believe that could be possible today with all of the varied external influences on stocks such as program trading. As markets and strategies evolve, so too must the trained eye of an LSI investor as spike patterns related to the formation of supply and demand imbalances evolve as well.

There is some very interesting independent work under way in the assessment of new investment strategies and securities using LSI charts. In addition to the three case studies outlined in Chapter 3, there are other existing trading and portfolio strategies that incorporate LSI charts. These range from simply being one of several tools used in the screening of stocks to investment strategies that are focused entirely on supply and demand imbalances. Some of the more intriguing studies involve the use of options and LSI charts. In contrast to the strategies discussed in the section, "Trading Options Using LSI Charts" in Chapter 3, LSI charts are being studied and applied directly to the option contracts themselves to discover correlations of supply and demand characteristics. Among international securities, LSI charts can be applied to virtually any stock, in any market, in any country. I have been amazed at the vivid patterns that develop with far greater frequency in Chinese stocks, for example, than in U.S. equities. Technical investors have worked with LSI charts to spot supply and demand imbalances ahead of chart breakouts to get a leg up on the multitude of other users of stock charts. LSI charts are also applicable to a range of additional strategies and securities, which remain an open frontier for the next generation of investors.

Taking all we have learned from the previous three chapters, investors should now be pretty familiar with the core LSI patterns that can generate investment performance in the market. Whether preferring conservative Stair-Step patterns for larger stocks or shooting for the moon with Ladders and Waves, the excitement truly comes in finding a stock with that "perfect pattern." I have spent many a night culling through hundreds of LSI charts before finding one prized gem that made it all worthwhile. But all eyes are different and my trained view is only what my own experience has led me to see. Far more interesting to me are the comments from colleagues who discover a particular nuance to LSI that I had never before seen or contemplated. Added to that is a nomenclature all of its own. A long-time friend always referred to the "smile line," a pattern that mirrored the rounded LSI line found in Bowls. I always enjoy hearing Ladder patterns being compared to such things as "rockets," and Wave patterns referred to as seismograph readings. In fact, the term "Wave" eventually evolved from that particular colleague's comment. One woman on a plane created a great deal of laughter after mistaking me for a physician catching up on heart EKGs as I was peering down at a group of LSI charts, spread out four to a page. With such varied interpretations, it is an enjoyable experience for me to ask an LSI user, "What is it that you see in the chart?"

An important fact to consider is that today countless investors look at stock charts. It is very difficult to gain an advantage in the market with so many people looking at the exact same image, which relegates many investors to being merely a follower of the herd. LSI charts for the first time brings supply and demand imbalances to life for investors seeking a differentiated way of looking at stocks. The ability to embark upon a new course and invest independently is thus once again an exciting possibility.

With this book finally in print after so many years of research and writing, I would now like to pass the torch on to the reader. Following two decades as a process available exclusively to institutional investors, LSI charts today are now accessible to individual investors through LSIcharts.com. There is so much more to explore and discover that it is my hope readers will assume the reins of LSI chart analysis from this point onward. Armed with the building blocks of supply and demand analysis, what hidden gems may you find by culling through the thousands of stocks that make up the market? What subtle patterns will you identify and deploy into action? And finally, "What is it that you see in the chart?" I now pass that question on to you!

Glossary

1-2 spike combination — An initial spike followed by a second, confirmatory spike that produces a buy signal under LSI analysis.

1-2-3 spike combination — A three spike combination occurring in a consecutive pattern that produces a buy signal. Usually associated with Ladder patterns.

Barb — Bullish chart feature resembling the barb of a fish hook. A barb is a small negative spike that occurs immediately after a positive spike but of a far lesser magnitude.

Bowl pattern — a turnaround pattern that features a reversal of the trajectory of the LSI line from negative to positive, resembling a rounded bowl. Bowls typically occur over several months to years.

Completion spike — A spike that completes a pattern such as the upward spike in a U pattern.

Decoupling — A movement on the LSI chart whereby the LSI line breaks away from its close proximity to an associated share price.

Delta — A widening area, or gap between the LSI line and share price
    Ascending — Bullish pattern. The LSI line moves higher at a faster rate than the share price to produce a widening gap between the two lines.
    Descending — Bearish pattern. The LSI line moves lower at a faster rate than the share price to produce a widening gap between the two lines.

Divergence — Movement of the LSI line in a manner opposite to that of the share price.
    Positive — Bullish pattern. Share price moves lower while the LSI line moves at a neutral to higher trajectory.
    Negative — Bearish pattern. Share price moves higher while the LSI line moves at a neutral to lower trajectory.

Institutional investor — An investment firm that manages a significant portfolio and has the ability to influence share prices through buying and selling activity.

Imbalances — Investment opportunities under LSI analysis. Periods where share supply and demand is not in equilibrium by virtue of heavy institutional buying or selling.

> **Demand** — Bullish indication. An undersupply of stock is created through heavy institutional buying.
> **Supply** — Bearish indication. An oversupply of stock is created through heavy institutional selling.
> **Equilibrium** — Neutral indication. Supply and demand are balanced.

Ladder pattern — An LSI power pattern featuring a consecutive sequence of spikes that occur over a condensed period of time to resemble the rungs of a ladder, in contrast to the more common Stair-Step. Ladders are characterized by three or more consecutive positive spikes beginning with a "1-2-3" combination.

LSI — Leedom Strength Indicator. LSI is an investment method that identifies the secretive and hidden influences on supply and demand created by institutional investors.

LSI algorithm — The engine of LSI charts that is responsible for producing the LSI line.

LSI chart — A chart featuring the LSI line and share price of a subject stock and used to identify supply and demand imbalances.

LSI line — A line produced by the LSI algorithm that represents the ongoing supply and demand characteristics of a subject stock. Patterns on the LSI line created by spikes allow investors to recognize supply and demand imbalances.

Mounding — A unique feature of Ladder patterns whereby the LSI line begins to plateau despite still experiencing positive spikes.

Pulse — A burst in volume and share price associated with the formation of LSI spikes.

Spike — A vertical upward or downward movement of the LSI line on an LSI chart which indicates institutional activity and serves as the building block of pattern formation.

> **Micro** — Very small magnitude spike. Defined as a spike 10% or less of the size of a primary spike.
> **Minor** — Small magnitude spike. Defined as a spike 50% or less of the size of a primary spike.
> **Primary** — Common spike. Defined as an average magnitude spike.
> **Major** — Large magnitude spike. Defined as a spike 150-200% of the size of a primary spike.
> **Spear** — Exceptionally large magnitude spike causing chart distortion.

Stair-Step pattern — The signature pattern of LSI charts featuring a series of spikes over time to resemble the upward or downward steps of a staircase.

> **Classic** — A highly uniform, smooth pattern of spikes on an LSI chart associated with ongoing supply or demand imbalances.
> **Aggressive** — A less uniform Stair-Step pattern caused by a higher frequency of spikes on an LSI chart and associated with more aggressive supply or demand imbalances.

U pattern — A turnaround pattern whose spikes feature a sharp downward and subsequent upward spike of equal magnitude to resemble that of the letter U. These patterns typically occur over weeks to years.

V pattern — An aggressive turnaround pattern whose spikes resemble that of the letter V. V patterns are rapid forming typically occurring over days to weeks.

Volume — The number of shares traded in a subject stock on a given day. Average volume is the number of shares that typically trade on a given day based on a trailing average.

Wave pattern — An LSI power pattern featuring sharp up-and-down gyrations of the LSI line that often resemble the s-waves and p-waves on a seismograph during an earthquake. Waves form with an initial primary spike followed by a series of positive and negative spikes occurring rapidly in a tight range and lasting on average a few weeks.

Wing pattern — An LSI power pattern notable for two features including a primary or major spike and the development of an ascending delta. Wing patterns tend to develop slowly and become increasingly powerful and are named for their resemblance to the outstretched wing of a bird.

> **Wing spike** — The primary or major spike that initiates a Wing pattern.

Company Index

Index

Made in the USA
Columbia, SC
29 April 2019